About the Book

Racing expert Irwin Stambler introduces you to the elite of drag racing
—the superpowered, nitro-burning Top Fuel Dragsters which are paired
in one-on-one competition in the final rounds of professional eliminations. You discover how this class of car offers one of the greatest
thrills in any sport. Mr. Stambler shows how the Top Fuelers represent
the pinnacle of engineering and human courage in the long saga of drag
racing. In this book are vivid portraits of some of the greatest Top Fuel
drivers. And then—vividly, dramatically—the author puts you behind
the wheel of one of these fabulous cars and has you drive through a
race.

TOP FUELERS
Drag Racing Royalty

Irwin Stambler

G.P. Putnam's Sons/New York

All photos are by Les Lovett, Official Photographer, NHRA.

Copyright © 1978 by Irwin Stambler
All rights reserved. Published
simultaneously in Canada by
Longman Canada Limited, Toronto.
PRINTED IN THE UNITED STATES OF AMERICA
10 up

Library of Congress Cataloging in Publication Data
Stambler, Irwin. Top fuelers.
Includes index.
SUMMARY: Introduces those elite cars of drag racing
known as Top Fuelers and profiles some of their top drivers.
1. Drag racing—Juvenile literature.
2. Automobile racing drivers—Biography—Juvenile
literature. [1. Drag racing. 2. Automobile
racing drivers. 3. Automobiles, Racing] I. Title.
GV1029.3.S72   796.7′2   77-13328
ISBN 0-399-61116-9 lib. bdg.

To Abe and Alice Seidman

Contents

TOP FUELERS

1

The Top Fuel Saga

The two elongated, lowslung vehicles sit there expectantly at the head of a long, black-asphalt runway that stretches a quarter of a mile into the distance. The brightly painted, wedge-shaped bodies, covered with a gaudy spectrum of names, numbers, and symbols, reflect the sunlight. Rumbles of ear-splitting sound pour from the vibrating engines with their long, sweeping exhaust stacks. Suspended above the rear, between the huge black tires of the odd looking cars, are stubby winglike surfaces.

The drivers' heads are barely visible, and what can be seen from the sidelines is somewhat unearthly. You can't make out faces—only bulbous helmets and special masks with large goggles covering the drivers' eyes. Occasionally the gloved hands of these earthbound astronauts trade signals with ground crews, who are carefully positioning the vehicles in the staging area just behind the central pole which with its dual string of lights, is called a Christmas Tree.

When all is ready, the two vehicles edge forward until their forward ends, supported by two skinny wheels that look as if they come from

After thundering down the quarter-mile strip at speeds of over 200 mph, two rocketing drag racers reach the finish line neck and neck.

bicycles, nudge an invisible electronic beam that actuates the Christmas Tree. The noise continues its unrelenting, pulsating patterns while the heat from the engines causes the air to shimmer like a desert mirage. For the drivers and the thousands of onlookers in stands lining the long, narrow roadway, the next few seconds seem to crawl by as the two gladiators rivet their gaze to the round, darkened shapes of the lower light bulbs.

Suddenly an amber glow appears in the next to last set, and the two vehicles roar into action. Both slice over the white starting line almost simultaneously as the lowest light flashes green. In a blur of motion, the two cars rocket down the straightaway, and a scant six seconds later one or the other zooms past the finish line—1,320 feet down the track—in triumph. To the onlookers at the starting line, the two cars have become faint specks in a wink of an eye, trailing billowing parachutes that are the only means of safely stopping these vehicles from dizzying speeds of 250 miles per hour (mph) and more within a few hundred feet.

That is what you see when the elite of drag racing, the superpowered, nitro-burning Top Fuel dragsters, are paired in one-on-one competition in the final rounds of professional eliminations. It is one of the great thrills in the field of auto racing. It represents the pinnacle of engineering accomplishment and human fearlessness in the long saga of drag racing.

The evolution of the Top Fuel dragster is in a straight line from the earliest beginnings of the sport. The primary principle of all drag purists is developing a four-wheel vehicle that could defeat other such vehicles by covering the quarter-mile course as quickly as possible. Maximum performance using internal combustion engine power has always been the prime goal in this class; everything in the system has been tailored toward this end. Hence the strange, elongated chassis, the use of special airfoils, the varying locations of the engine—originally, ahead of the driver and, in the 1970s, behind the cockpit.

By contrast, the two other main Professional categories of dragging

13

The burnout, a key prerace maneuver, sends up swirling clouds of smoke and vapor while getting tires and track clean and ready for high-acceleration starts.

have certain inherent restrictions that make it harder for drivers and designers to squeeze further dramatically higher speeds and elapsed times. In Funny Cars, for instance, a prime requirement is that the plastic body, fitted over the dragster chassis, has the look and dimensions of standard-production automobiles. That naturally limits the chassis size. In the third category, Pro Stock, the race vehicle must be a Detroit-model car, although racing teams can carefully assemble and hone the engine and component systems for maximum efficiency. Thus Pro Stock top speeds are far below either Funnies or Top Fuelers.

Of course, in drag racing's infancy, there was nothing very fancy about the models. Essentially, the cars were just stock designs—roadsters, coupes, sedans—which young enthusiasts carefully maintained and adjusted for short, fast-acceleration races against one another. The sport just sort of happened, growing out of impromptu challenges of one driver by another on side streets or back country roads. For many years drag racing was a haphazard, amateur entertainment that slowly became formalized in response to growing opposition of police and local citizens to the dangers of street racing.

The main incubator for drag racing was California. There, in the 1930s, groups of car fanciers began meeting to test their skills in remote areas, such as off-road regions of the Mojave Desert. The scope of those events grew until throngs of drivers and onlookers assembled regularly for meets. The sport, which began to spread to all corners of the country, was curtailed by World War II. But when the war ended, drag racing returned to the fore with even more vigor. There still were no vehicles built for the sport. Participants usually took old model cars and fitted them out with souped-up engines, mainly flathead Fords and some six-cylinder General Motors designs, for higher performance.

With more cars on the road, the public concern over the dangers of uncontrolled hot-rod racing brought cries for outlawing the sport. For a while it appeared this might happen. But there were many conscientious and far-seeing people in drag racing who realized the logic of the public concern. They soon began to look for ways to organize drag racing to preserve its good points while eliminating the objectionable.

Before long drag strips began to be set aside in cities and towns across the United States. There the drivers could race their newest, hottest creations under rules that applied to all involved and under conditions assuring maximum safety for both drivers and the community. After a while, as these tracks grew in size and facilities, they provided exciting surroundings for drivers and car builders. They also gradually became a major lure for people who didn't drag race at all, but enjoyed watching an exciting sporting event.

The year 1951 is memorable in drag-racing history. It was the year when the pioneer organizing-sanctioning body was born. Called the National Hot Rod Association (NHRA), it was created in Southern California by a group that included Wally Parks, still president of the organization in the mid 1970s. The NHRA set up categories and rules and, in the next few years, arranged for nationwide tours of expert racers to show the country what the new sport was all about. Afterward, other sanctioning groups came into existence, such as the American Hot Rod Association (AHRA) and the International Hot Rod Association (IHRA).

Another development in 1951 was the invention of the advanced type of racer called a slingshot, which was the catalyst paving the way for the all-out top-fuel competition of later decades. The innovator who brought this about was a young Los Angeles hot-rodder named Mickey Thompson. Mickey previously had followed the usual route of drag enthusiasts, taking an old Ford Model-A car and stripping it to the frame before putting in an upgraded flathead Ford engine.

It occurred to Mickey that designs of that kind had gone just about as far as they could go. It was all but impossible to go much faster than the then record of 119 mph or to move elapsed times to the lower 10-second region.

He thought about it and came up with a range of variations he thought would pay off. He took his cue to some extent from the aviation field where going faster is related to making the plane lighter. He decided to buy some metal tubing used for plane wing struts and make a new chassis by welding lengths of tubing together. In airplane design, proper distribution is important; to achieve this in his new car, Mickey shifted the location of the engine back to the normal driver's position and placed the seat behind the rear wheels. The rear wheels were brought closer together by narrowing the cockpit area so there was just enough room for him to squeeze in. In addition, for better traction, he had the tires recapped without tread, the original "slicks." The wheelbase of the car was 96 inches and the tire width 5½ inches.

When he had the chance to demonstrate his new design in early 1951, it soon picked up the nickname slingshot. Like a slingshot, the maximum weight was to the rear. And, as soon as the clutch was dropped, the car streaked into action as if propelled by a slingshot.

"Everybody laughed at my first slingshot," Thompson recalled a few years ago. "At first the officials wouldn't let me run it. They claimed it was too dangerous. When I finally got my chance at the strip on the old Santa Ana blimp base, I opened their eyes. On the first run, I hit 127 mph and was clocked in 10.25 e.t. [elapsed time], both new records."

The slingshot quickly became the standard for top-quality racing as the best drivers began to build steadily improved versions. The new advance in performance played a role in the rapidly increasing popularity of drag racing that helped increase paying customers at newly built tracks around the country and soon made it possible for expert racers to earn a living from the sport.

The NHRA helped focus attention on the best exponents of drag racing by setting up its first National Championship event at Great Bend, Kansas, in 1955. The first National Champion crowned at that meet was Calvin Rice, who hit a top speed in his Dragster-Merc of 143 mph and had a best e.t. of 10.30 seconds. The Nationals moved to Kansas City the following year, shifted to Oklahoma City for 1957 and 1958, then to Detroit for two years. In 1961 the Nationals moved to Indianapolis Raceway Park in Indianapolis, where it has remained ever since. For many years the Nationals was the only world champion meet NHRA sponsored, and it still is one of the two or three crowns most sought after by drivers.

As in all large scale meets many different classes, both Professional and Sportsman, or amateur groupings, were run from the start. But the top attractions, from the beginning until the Funny Car challenge of the late 1960s, were the unlimited dragsters descended from the original slingshot.

You get an idea of the wide range of options available to a drag enthusiast when you realize the main sanctioning bodies have rules covering anywhere from 70 or 80 to over 100 different classifications. Taking the improved stock car class alone, called Super Stocks, the NHRA rulebook covered some 40 different classes in the mid 1970s with the variations based on car size, type of engine, transmission design, and the like. Still other Sportsman classes include modified production, street roadsters and gas coupes and sedans. However, there are only three Professional categories today: Top Fuel, Funny Cars and Pro Stock; and for a long time in Class AA there was only Top Fuel.

In the mid 1950s the unlimited dragsters became known as top fuelers because of the use of the superpowerful propellants derived from a chemical compound called nitromethane. It was with such mixtures that Don Garlits amazed the drag-racing world with the first speeds of over 170 mph and elapsed times well below 10 seconds. However, by the late 1950s it became obvious to sanctioning bodies that dragster design just wasn't able to cope with the tremendous horsepower which could be gained with improved nitro mixtures. So nitro was banned as long as that kind of fuel exceeded the capability of the car. For a number of years the top cars ran on gas.

Meanwhile, racers were experimenting with all kinds of design ad-

Jerry Ruth has some anxious moments as his dragster executes an unscheduled "wheelie."

vances, developing better, more stable chassis arrangements, improving transmission components, finding tire systems that would give greater traction. One of the major changes that came into vogue at the start of the 1960s was the longer wheelbase. It made the dragster look weirder to fans, but it made the driver's task simpler and safer.

Mickey Thompson explained the reason for the move to Los Angeles *Times* reporter Shav Glick: "Suppose a top fueler weighs 1,250 pounds sitting on the line, static, the rear end weighs 1,000 pounds and the front end 250. When you let the clutch out, the weight transfers to the rear, making it weigh about 1,240 and the front end 10. The delicate decision is not to overdo the weight transfer and have the front end fly up in the air. When the cars had shorter wheelbases, they needed extra weight in the front. It became more practical to extend the front end."

As a result, wheelbases went from 90–100 inches to 230 inches. This helps insure that the dragster will keep moving straight ahead, rather than flipping over or spinning. A short wheelbase car has a tendency to do both if the driver loses control momentarily.

Of course, even with a long chassis model, under certain conditions the front end can flip up. Stunt drivers will do this to entertain the crowd. But those spectacular "wheelies" have no place in an actual race or qualifying run. When a dragster is in that odd position, it is losing speed and time. The object of drag racing still is to beat your opponent to the finish line, and all professional drivers know that calls for keeping the four wheels down on the ground.

The long wheelbase brought other gains in car design. For example, the front suspension could be done away with. The long tubular frame accomplished the same task previously done by springs, shocks, and torsion bars since it twisted and flexed to meet the conditions of the track.

Starting with the first slingshot, the goal also has been to cut down on dragster weight while upping the power output of the engine. "Before 1951," Thompson told Glick, "the theory was that the car with the most

20

cubic inches would be fastest. I decided that a light car, with less cubic inches could go faster than a heavy one with more power." Using light-weight aircraft-type tubing was one approach. Thompson took it a step further later on by drilling holes in the tubing and other metal parts, where it could be done without reducing strength, to reduce weight.

Thus where a typical passenger car of today might weigh 4,000 pounds, the top-fuel dragster tips the scale at only a quarter of that. On the other hand, the almost 500-cubic-inch engines of the late 1970s turn out 1,500 horsepower or more compared to 250 or 300 hp in a conventional automobile. Light weight is also vital in that powerful modern dragging engine. Year by year, as the 1970s went by, one engine component after another was switched from steel to the less dense, but very strong, aluminum alloys. By the late 1970s almost every winning driver used what amounted to an all-aluminum engine.

Tire design also made a big difference, playing as important a role as higher horsepower engines in bringing the dazzling rises in speed and estimated time of the 1960s and 1970s. Even though Mickey Thompson was using treadless tires in his early cars, most racers didn't use them because tire companies didn't provide tires specially designed for drag needs. In the 1960s, though, that changed.

Don Prudhomme outlined the changes for a reporter: "If any one thing caused the big strides of the last decade, it has been tire development. Until about 1965, we were experimenting mainly with treads, but then a small company in Watertown, Massachusetts, called M & H, started to build slicks specifically for dragsters. First they went to a 7-inch tread which seemed really wide. And then the big companies like Goodyear got in the business and experimented with wider and wider tires. The wider a tire is, the softer and 'gummier' it can be for extra traction."

By the mid 1970s the huge rear slicks on a top-fuel dragster consisted of an outer tire and an inner liner. The inner tire is inflated to a pressure of about 50 pounds, while the outer section only carries about

4 pounds. That is why, if you look at a dragster in the pits or at rest on the line behind the staging area, its tires will look soft and wrinkled.

The idea is that, as the friction heat from the car's high-speed movement feeds into the slick tire surface, it causes the material to expand. By the time the vehicle hurtles past the finish line, the tire will have a diameter 7 or 8 inches greater than at the start.

"This," says Prudhomme, "gives a car the effect of shifting without having to touch the gears. The centrifugal force makes the tire grow, and as it grows, it increases the horsepower."

Of course, you can't change one thing in as sensitive a system as a 200-mph-plus dragster without carefully developing everything else to maximum efficiency. Whether it's an engine piston, a drive shaft, or a wheel, the parts must be carefully studied to ensure that all work well together and the components must be precisely made from the highest quality materials. That is one reason why only professionals with plenty of resources move into the Top Fuel class these days and stay there.

The equipment needed to compete in such fast company costs many thousands of dollars. A good engine made by a top engine builder like Keith Black Racing Engines, Ed Pink Racing Engine, or Donavan Racing Engines will cost $8,000, $9,000, or more. When body-building specialists like John Buttera, Don Long, or Kent Fuller contract to fabricate a top-fuel chassis in their shops, they expect to be paid equally well for their skills. Just buying a new digger can cost upwards of $20,000 and the race team still must take into account operating costs for fuel, spare parts, a truck transporter for the dragster, and the like.

In recent decades many organizations have evolved to supply the needs of drag racers. Besides the prime engine and chassis builders, there are a host of other specialized firms providing subsystems that go into the major assemblies—things like superchargers, specially ground cams, fuel injection systems, wheels, headers. To name just a few of these companies: Venolia, for forged racing pistons and rings; Edelbrock, intake manifolds; Cragar, wheels, headers, and ignitions; Hays, gaskets; Iskenderian, ground cams; Lenco, transmissions. You can tell which firm's equipment is used by a favorite driver by reading the inscriptions painted all over the dragster body.

The rise of such a group of skilled suppliers helped maintain the steady advance in dragster performance throughout the 1960s and 1970s. The years of experience represented by the technical people and mechanics of those concerns made it possible for them to turn the ideas of racing teams into workable reality in short periods of time. It also provided important sources of suggestions for still further improvements of car designs.

All these factors helped make the "expert" views of the mid 1950s obsolete in less than a decade. Wise people in 1955–56 emphasized that there was no way a vehicle could be catapulted 1,320 feet from a standing start to speeds much over 160 mph or with elapsed times below eight seconds. Before 10 years had passed, top speeds had gone up well over 30 per cent, and within the next 10 years, the awesome 250-mph peak had been scaled, with drivers such as Shirley Muldowney, Gary Beck, and Don Garlits shooting for 255 or 260.

Maximum speed or minimum e.t.'s may not determine who wins a drag race, however. In fact, speeds have no bearing on race results by themselves, although the sanctioning bodies carefully monitor them for world record purposes. And even e.t.'s are final arbiters only in the preliminaries where the lowest e.t.'s are used in selecting the 16 or 32 drivers for the eliminator finals. In eliminations winning or losing is determined by which car crosses the finish line first. It is possible for a car to have a lower e.t. than a rival in the next lane and still lose the race. That would happen, for instance, if the faster car left the starting line fractions of a second after the slower one.

This doesn't mean a driver can ignore making his or her car run as fast as possible. Unless a top fueler is capable of getting speeds around the 240- or 250-mph level and low e.t.'s, the vehicle won't stand much chance of beating the superstar competition at national championship events.

Despite the amazing gains in vehicle performance to the point where dragsters cover the quarter mile at speeds four or five times those of a typical freeway driver, it doesn't mean a reduction in safety. In fact, most drivers agree that the many advances actually have made drag racing safer.

This was one reason Don Garlits gave for his continuing in the sport even though he was an "old man" by the standards of other sports. "I've thought about retiring hundreds of times," he told the Los Angeles *Times* in 1972, "but why should I? The dragsters we're building now are so much more sophisticated, there is no comparison to the old 'slingshots' of 5 or 10 years ago. You needed a lot of plain strength to hold those on the track, but the new fuelers are much easier to handle and they allow you freedom to concentrate on driving without worrying about wrestling with them. I can drive for another five years and maybe longer."

Which proved a good prophesy. Five years later, he still was competing at the top levels. In 1975 he had his greatest year ever, winning the championship of not only the NHRA, but the IHRA as well. And in 1977 he started the year by barely losing the Winternationals in the final race.

Garlits, of course, helped make the prophesy come true by perfecting the rear-engine dragster, a breakthrough of the 1970s equal in importance to Mickey Thompson's 1951 slingshot design. The result is obvious if you go to the track these days. You can count on your fingers the top fuelers that have the engine ahead of the driver, where it always was placed in the 1960s. And the few cars that do use front engines have a hard job keeping up with the steady stream of rear-engine jobs, which keep moving into the staging lanes during qualifying and eliminations.

It took some getting used to, even by veteran drivers like Don Prudhomme. But the Snake agreed, "It changed everything, but it is definitely safer." Still, he said, "it's hard to get the feel of the engine when it's behind you. Before, you could check it visually. It was sitting right in your lap. But now you have to forget about the engine. You've got to

Fire! That's one thing you don't want when you're strapped into what has been called "a bomb with a six-second fuse." Luckily for driver Marvin Graham, these flames were snuffed out seconds later.

assume it's ok and concentrate on taking off straight."

The new engine demonstrated again the interrelationship of everything in drag racing, including the track layout itself. Though having the engine in the rear provided protection for the driver in case the engine caught on fire, exploded, or spewed out broken parts, it initially added danger if the car went sideways. Larry Dixon, still driving a front-engine digger in the late 1970s, pointed out, "I like having the engine in front, because then my seat is back between the rear wheels. If you go to the guard rail side, those slicks are just like big rubber bumpers. A friend of mine started to roll in a rear-engine car and he went right under the guard rail and was badly injured."

The problem was that the guard rails were not set up for the new systems. But major tracks now have installed new rail systems, so rear-engine cars can't slide under them. With that change, almost all drivers feel more comfortable and safer with the engine behind them.

Steady improvement in safety equipment has matched other changes in the dragster systems. In the early 1960s, drivers still wore little more than a black leather jacket and boots even though speeds already were approaching 200 mph. Several of the greatest drivers spent months in hospitals recovering from severe burns caused by accidents or fires.

Since then changes have come rapidly. Racing rules for all major meets require that every driver wear special fireproof suits, gloves, boots, and face masks. The suits are carefully tested before leaving the factory to make sure that even with 1,850 degrees of heat outside, enough to melt many metals, and pressures of 85 pounds per square inch, the inside temperature can't exceed 180°F for 10 seconds or more. The sanctioning bodies also require that competing top-fuel cars be equipped with special seat-belt shoulder installations that absorb energy in case the car starts to flip or roll, but that can be easily unfastened by the driver so he can escape once the car comes to rest.

All cars now have an on-board fire extinguishing system which the driver can actuate at any point in the run. The extinguishers use a du

Pont chemical called Freon, a nontoxic, colorless and odorless substance, which after release into the atmosphere, renders the air unable to support combustion when only 4 percent saturation level is reached. Special parachute arresting systems also are a must, and those drag chutes are made of high strength materials which can't rip under high airloads that press against them when the car is moving at well over 250 mph.

Those items and more besides have made drag racing a pretty safe sport, despite the severe operating conditions. At a track you might see instances where cars go out of control and hit the guard rail at 220 or 230 mph or roll over and over spilling twisted metal and oil across the asphalt—or even have the engine explode sending fireballs of flame into the air. Luckily, those things don't happen often. When they do, in almost every instance the driver walks away—shaken, perhaps, but unhurt.

And that racer is sure to be back soon, often to make new imprints in the record books, helping to push drag-racing horizons to impressive new levels. Thus the drag-racing fans of the 1970s could cheer as the top-fuel drivers moved the e.t.'s all the way down from the sixes and sevens into the fives.

A familiar sight at drag strips: lines of quiescent dragsters and their push cars await the call to move into the staging lanes.

2

Into the Five's

In any sporting event fans attend partly to see a favorite performer or team and partly to root home a winner. But everyone hopes that something special will happen, that maybe a new record will be set. In track it might be a new pole vault height or a new sprint mark. In football you might be present when a new rushing record is set. In baseball there are days like Henry Aaron's becoming a new home run king. But in drag racing the prime hope is a Guinness-book elapsed time achievement.

Setting a record isn't easy in any sport. And in drag racing it is considerably more difficult than most. A track, football, or baseball star doesn't have to risk flaming infernos or sudden machinery failure at several hundred miles an hour. Nor is one faced with the exacting, expensive demands of squeezing extra performance out of already strained equipment. So, in a sense, each extra split second sliced off the time taken to rocket down the 1,320 feet of a drag strip takes much more preparation and patient concentration than almost any other accomplishment.

Still, the record books show a steady decrease in e.t.'s over the relatively short history of professional drag racing. In the 1950s, times of 11 and 12 seconds were considered excellent. When champions like Don Garlits, Jack Chrisman, Norm Weekly, James Warren, and Pete Robinson brought the figures down in the 1960s to levels of 9, 8, and then 7 plus seconds, many observers thought everyone had "gone about as far as they could go." Then Tom McEwen hit 6.97 in his McEwen and Johnson Chrysler-powered fuel dragster and a new scramble was on. From then until the early 1970s, top-fuel racers nicked away at the record until everyone started wondering whether the next barrier, "the 5's," might fall.

In truth, moving from the 12's into the 6's, almost a 100 percent improvement in roughly a decade, was an amazing accomplishment. It can be compared to such progress as going from subsonic to supersonic speeds in aviation or propelling vehicles to high enough accelerations to escape earth's gravity and reach outer space. While those advances were made by large groups of engineers and scientists who could use massive experimental facilities, drag racers essentially had to depend on seat-of-the-pants experience. Drag-racing teams had to score their breakthroughs on budgets in the thousands of dollars, while aviation and space groups had almost unlimited resources amounting to hundreds of millions of dollars.

The drag-racing expert couldn't afford fancy wind tunnels or special materials-testing equipment. For the most part it was a trial and error process. Change this a little, try it out. Change that a bit, try it out. The driver usually was his own "test pilot," daring death or injury each time he moved to the head of the drag strip with a major change in engine, chassis, or other component.

For those reasons the record gains made were, in the 1950s, mainly through brute strength rather than subtle changes based on such things as aerodynamics. When Don Garlits startled the drag world with the first top speeds of over 170 mph, his vehicles looked like ugly ducklings. But he was one of the best manipulators of special fuel mixtures. Though he hadn't been to engineering school or taken advanced courses in chemistry, he was a born technician. Intuitively he realized that developing fuels which could drive pistons down with maximum output per pound of fuel would mean much higher speeds and times. He depended on very volatile mixtures of fuels like those used in rockets rather than in cars.

Before long the basic energy system in every first-rank dragster was based on such propellants. However, drag experts moved too fast in squeezing more juice from high energy chemicals. It got to the point that those fuels had performance which exceeded the capability of the drag vehicle. After dangerous accidents occurred, sanctioning bodies banned them for some years and ordered conventional gasoline substituted. So the designation of the class for a number of years was AA/D.

Even then the racing fraternity adjusted to the new restrictions and began improving chassis, controls, and the like, which helped provide impressive performances with gas. In 1960 Joe Tucci set an NHRA record of 9.06 e.t., and it wasn't too long before Jack Chrisman in his Howard Cam Special cut into the 8's for the first time with an 8.97 in May, 1961. He lowered it several more times to 8.78 (8.61) before giving way to new marks, first by Glen Ward and then by Jim Nelson (8.59).

The gains in the overall dragster opened the door for high energy fuel once more. Characteristically it was Don Garlits who started that revolution with his Dodge-powered Swamp Rat. In February, 1963, he roared to a smart 8.24 seconds in Pomona, California. From that time to this, the Top Fuel class has been designated AA/FD. The introduction of superchargers and other innovations helped keep the fans on edge waiting for still another superperformance. The racing stars didn't disappoint them, moving the e.t. down almost month by month until it suddenly burst into the 7's in mid 1964. The first NHRA contestant to reach that level officially was Bobby Vodnik, who rocketed to a 7.96 e.t. in Dick Belfatti's Chrysler-engined "Shadow" in May, 1964.

As 1964 went by several drivers took turns at hitting the momentary plateau of 7.91 with Zane Shubert doing it first in June followed soon after by Connie Swingle (in a Don Garlits digger) and Paul Sutherland. But once more it took the old master Garlits to knock the mark down sharply when he zipped to a stunning time of 7.78 seconds at Island Dragway in the course of shattering the 200 mph barrier with his historic 201.34.

The name of the game, as he emphasized again, was knowing how to concoct the witch's brew of chemical fluids which could squeeze a little more horsepower out of the eight-cylinder engine and matching that with dragster system alignments. And when Garlits or any race team comes up with an improvement, it tries to keep the composition from the competition as long as possible.

As Garlits told a reporter in 1964, "I used to mix the fuel right at the strip, but there are too many spies around trying to find out what I'm doing with it. Now I mix it privately. It's all quite complex for anyone outside the sport. Even people in the sport don't know what I've done to reach 200. Oh, they say they know, but they don't. For instance, the fuel. They don't know how I'm getting the proper balance. Actually, the big thing is imagination. You see, there are six major factors: the supercharger, the pistons, the camshafts, the gear ratio, the tires, and the fuel. It's the combinations you use. For each factor there are, say, 25 different combinations. I interpret this all as just imagination."

No matter how an innovator tries to keep new knowledge to himself (or herself), other race teams catch up pretty fast. Garlits' 7.78 held for a while, but within a year, drivers like Danny Ongais (7.59), Buddy Cortines (7.54) and Don Westerdale (7.47) smoked their way into the record book. Then the pace slowed and Westerdale's mark was untouched for over a year.

Just when everyone thought e.t. progress had hit a plateau, James Warren started the ball rolling again by his blistering run in September, 1966, in a Chrysler-powered Warren & Coburn AA/FD at Irwindale,

**Trapped air strains against high-strength parachute material as two high-speed
racers start to slow down after a blazing duel down the quarter-mile strip.**

California, that chopped almost 10 seconds off the old record to a new low of 7.38. His feeling of elation didn't last out the month, however, for Vic Brown in a Chrysler-powered Greitz & Greer machine cut the best e.t. to 7.26 at Bristol, Tennessee.

Drag fans started to wonder whether the 6's might be within reach. It was hard to believe that only about two and a half years earlier, a low eight-second run was considered phenomenal. But despite the torrid attack on the e.t. bastions, many were skeptical that the steady reduction could be maintained. The argument waxed hot and heavy into early 1966 as several drivers made runs that approached Brown's 7.26, but none lowered it.

Then along came Pete Robinson in his "Tinker Toy" at Phenix City, Alabama, who came within hailing distance of the 6's with a phenomenal 7.08. His AA/FD used a Ford engine, becoming the first Ford powerplant to set a new e.t. record in the 1960s. In fact, the record book shows that this achievement broke a total domination of e.t. breakthroughs by Chrysler Corporation engines which went all the way back to the AA/D gas-dragster period of 1960–1961 when Chevys reigned supreme.

With Robinson's feat, it became obvious the 6's would be reached. It was just a matter of time and place. The wait proved a short one. The very next month word flashed across the country thaat a new champion had been crowned. It was the likable Southern California ace Tom McEwen who did it, driving his blown Chrysler-powered McEwen & Johnson AA/FD to a 6.97 before a wildly cheering crowd at Carlsbad, California. (McEwen, nicknamed "Mongoose," gained national attention in the early 1970s during a series of special Funny Car match races with Don "Snake" Prudhomme, races that solidified Funnies as a prime competitor to Fuel Dragsters for top Professional drag classification.)

Hardly had the ink dried in the record book when Pete Robinson gunned his "Tinker Toy" to an equal 6.97 at another southern track, Palmetto Raceway. The 6.97 timing was to remain the record in AA/

FD's for two years making the next milestone, the 5's, seem ever farther in the distant future with each passing month. However, 6.97 did not remain the absolute pinnacle during that time. In August, 1967, Hank Westmoreland accomplished the unusual feat of breaking on top in a Sportsman-type category. At York, Pennsylvania, he sat behind the wheel of a Chrysler-powered BB/Fuel Dragster and piloted it to a remarkable 6.88. In all of NHRA history from 1960 on that was the only time a non–Pro-class driver established either an elapsed time or a top speed record. All other records to this day have gone to AA/D or AA/FD vehicles.

During the long hiatus in new e.t.'s, there was no lack of hot competition among superb drivers and race teams. Though winning the big ones was the primary goal, there was plenty of enthusiasm for trying new fuel mixtures or dragster system modifications that might slice a few more seconds or miles per hour off the existing levels.

As Garlits once noted, "I like to hit new highs. I feel it's part of my job. I like to exceed the strip records so that when I go away from there the fans will say, 'Well, we were out at the drag center and Big Daddy broke both ends of the strip record.' This sticks in their minds. In other words I've been hired to leave them breathless, right? I'm the professional, the hired killer who's supposed to have done all those things. And if you come there and don't live up at least partially to your reputation, guys get to thinking, well, it's just a whole bunch of phony advertising. If you're billed as Big Daddy, the National Champion, 240 miles an hour, World's Fastest Dragster, you should do something that's exceptional. And I'm going to drive that way."

In different ways all top drivers express the same thoughts. One puts it this way: "Naturally you always want to do your best. If you don't have pride in your work, you'll never get to be top dog in it. And the cheers from the crowd help, even though you can't hear a thing but the boom and crackle of the engine when you're strapped down in that tight cocoon. But you know it's there, particularly if you're running well, and that helps make the adrenalin flow to try to do even better."

But the faster the vehicles went, the tougher it became to dent the laws of nature a bit more. During the last half of 1967 all the way through to late spring of 1969, the greatest drivers pushed the top speeds up, but no one could dent the e.t. mark. In September, 1967, for instance, Mel Van Niewenhuise clocked 227.85 at Arlington, Washington, and James Warren equaled it at Irwindale. A year later John Mulligan moved the official record to 229.59 in his Chrysler-powered Beebe & Mulligan four wheeler at Orange County Raceway. But no one could knock even a split second off the time.

Meanwhile, the Funnies kept closing in, even though the cut-down length of those special plastic-bodied dragsters made it technically more difficult to make them go faster. With each year of Funnies existence as a top Pro class, drivers like Gene Snow, Don Schumacher, and new contenders from the top-fuel ranks like Tom McEwen and Don Prudhomme kept running faster. In the mid 1960s, the e.t.'s were in the 8's; as the decade drew to a close, the times were moving into the low 7's. It didn't seem likely that the Funnies could actually surpass the superdragsters of Top Fuel in e.t. With the greater design leeway top fuelers had in length, tire size, and other parameters, it seemed they always should stay ahead of the upstart challengers that were gaining so much fan attention.

Then, suddenly, the ball started moving again. The northwest champion, Jerry Ruth, moved out on his home course in Bremerton, Washington, in May, 1969, and brought the crowd to its feet with a dazzling performance. He didn't lower the record a tenth of a second, but twice that, establishing a new standard in his Chrysler-powered AA/FD of 6.68. In a short time a flurry of new marks were set. The name on everyone's lips in Top Fuel from the fall of 1969 to the fall of 1970 was Tom Raley. Driving his Jim & Allison Lee Chrysler digger, the entry out of The Plains, Virginia, was the pride of the northeast, winning NHRA Top Fuel honors for that division both years. Along the way to

The start of the race that produced the first under-six-seconds elapsed time. The late Mike Snively, nearest the camera, takes the green against Vic Brown. Snively flashed past the finish line in 5.97 seconds, but lost the race because he left the starting line after Brown.

top placing in many meets, he cut into the e.t. record twice, once in September, 1969, when he made 6.64 at Atco, New Jersey, and again in October, 1970, when he moved out to a 6.51 at Dallas, Texas.

The improvements in e.t. weren't coming fast enough to suit many in the field, though. While top-fuel experts struggled to gain slightly better performance, Funny Car teams were making dramatic strides in their category. In 1970 Don Schumacher almost broke the 6's barrier, hitting a notable 7.001. Fears began to rise that Funnies might do the impossible and equal or surpass Top Fuelers in performance. If that happened, many sports writers conjectured, the long-time king of dragsters might be dethroned. Already, in some parts of the country, fans were asking track owners for more Funny Car events and indicating a lessening of interest in Top Fuel.

Funny Car star Gene Snow could see both the plastic-bodied breed and Top Fuelers getting down to the low 6's. To go further, though, he looked for breakthroughs in engine technology. Talking about that in January, 1971, he predicted, "It won't be with today's engine. I think we've about reached our limit in speed and elapsed time with today's power plants. Right now we are at the ultimate, and it's very difficult to pick up a tenth of a second."

Others agreed with him, but they reckoned without the inventiveness of top-fuel king Don Garlits. Almost at the same time Snow was discussing engine concepts, Garlits was taking the wraps off his new rear-engined Wynn's Jammer at the AHRA Grand American meet at Lions Drag Strip. Sneaking a look at it, Don Prudhomme exclaimed, "Garlits, you've got to be kidding!"

But it was no joke when Garlits put his foot to the floor in competition. He tore down the strip at 225.25 mph and 6.56 sec. He was short of Raley's record of 6.53, but the important thing was that he proved the rear-engined design could be made stable and could turn out top speeds and e.t.'s. Even though Don lost in the finals that time and shortly after in Orange County's Raceways' All-Pro meet to Gary

38

Cochran's conventional slingshot, the writing was on the wall. Knowledgeable observers could see a revolution brewing. Shav Glick of the Los Angeles *Times* wrote, "Prediction: Don Garlits rear-engine top-fuel dragster will have the same impact on drag racing that Jack Brabham's rear-engine Cooper Climax has on Indianapolis racing."

After his January efforts Garlits told reporters, "That's the most pleasurable ride I ever had. It's just great out in front of all that noise. There's no fear of flying parts. The water, clutch dust, and oil don't blur your goggles.

"Ever since my accident last March [when a transmission failure took off part of his right foot], I've been thinking and trying to figure out a way to be safer and still go faster. We had to go faster. The Funny Cars were catching up with us.

"I couldn't figure any way but a rear engine. Sure, no one had ever made one work, but then I'd never even tried. And to be safer you had to put all that noise and machinery someplace else. Behind the driver was the only place."

During the season everywhere Don went he created a sensation. Fans and competing drivers alike crowded around the car in the pits. The other drivers hardly could suppress their enthusiasm as they carefully scanned the Jammer to see how Don had done it. Though they all were brave individuals, many longed for the clear view ahead the new dragster promised. They looked forward for relief from the occasional worries that came from staring at that pounding monster of an engine.

And Don was making believers of them by winning, too. He began by taking the NHRA Winternationals in January and added the Springnationals laurel at Dallas International Motor Speedway. He didn't break the e.t. record, but he was sure that was coming. He had a new mark to shoot at: in June, Rick Ramsey in a front-engined Chrysler eased it down to 6.51. Three months later Garlits pushed that aside with an amazing 6.26 at Gainesville, Florida. That just about clinched it. The rear-engined dragster would be the kingpin of racing from 1972 on.

39

Perennial record breaker Big Daddy Don Garlits missed the chance to be first into the fives, but he made up for it by becoming the first driver to crack 250 mph, simultaneously setting a new e.t. milestone of 5.63.

And indeed it was. As soon as the racing clan came out of its short winter hibernation to start running in California, the programs were crammed with notations of drivers entering AA/FD-RE's.

The last gasp in the record books for front-engine diggers came in early 1972 when Tony Nancy in his Dodge-powered "Loner" became the first to go over 230 mph, hitting a pace of 233.60 through the speed traps at Long Beach, California. His e.t., though, while under 7 seconds, fell short of the record. From then on, whether for speed or e.t., it was all rear-engine country.

In April, 1972, Clayton Harris in Jack McKay's Chrysler-powered "New Dimension" posted a 6.25 time at Suffolk, Virginia. A month later that was eclipsed by a Gene Snow prepared rear-engine job driven by Chip Woodall. The Dodge-engined vehicle sped to a 6.24 e.t. during a run at New England Dragway. Not to be outdone, Clayton Harris came back in July at Long Beach, California, scoring a heady 6.15 e.t. in his "New Dimension."

Almost in hushed tones, many fans, after looking at those times, started thinking out loud about the fives. Could it be that still another once remote barrier would be crossed? What about all those equations that once indicated there was only so much performance that could be coaxed from an engine? Though history had already demonstrated that all the so-called barriers proved to be imaginary, it was hard to believe the fives might give way as the sixes once had. Even if it was to happen, many concluded, it probably wouldn't take place until another racing year started and the experts had a month or two to rework equipment and refine everything.

So no one was expecting too much "super" at the final NHRA event on the 1972 calendar, the Supernationals at Ontario Motor Speedway, other than the usual tough competition and some good e.t.'s in the low sixes.

But there was a forewarning of momentous events to come during qualifying. One driver after the other streaked down the strip in what usually was the individual's best time ever. Indy Nationals champion Gary Beck came in with a 6.11, well below the record, and still was only third when qualifying was over. Surpassing him was Mike Snively in a new digger built by "Diamond Jim" Annin with a 6.10 and Colorado's Ed Renck took the top spot with a 6.09. There was even a possible lower run, a 6.03 by Gary Southern of Glendora, California, which was disallowed by the officials. Before the final field was chosen, the "bump" spot was a fantastic 6.26.

When the eliminations were ready to start that Sunday, there was a feeling in the air that history might be made. All the qualifying times were excellent. Significantly, too, for the first time at a major NHRA event, there were no front engines in sight. All 16 of the finalists had the engine where Don Garlits had demonstrated it should be—behind the driver. Ironically, Don himself wasn't there. He had passed up the Supernationals to take part in the "Turkey Trot" drags back home in Florida.

In round one the times were good, but still too high for the fans. Clayton Harris, the reigning e.t. record holder, won his match with the low round e.t. of 6.13. Things became even more interesting in round two. Don Moody in his Cerny & Moody Chrysler-powered digger turned back his opponent with the fastest ever statistics of 6.005 e.t. and 232.55 mph. When Moody came back to the staging lane for round three, the fans were in an uproar. "Into the fives, Don," some shouted, yelling themselves hoarse in hopes of seeing that epic achievement. When the green glowed, Moody came out fast on what seemed like a sub–six-second pace, but as soon as he saw he had beaten Carl Olson, he shut down and coasted home to a "slow" 6.01 as the crowd groaned.

Then came Mike Snively versus Vic Brown. After the disappointment over Moody's cautiousness, many onlookers felt the race was anticlimactic. Snively was a fine driver, but he was using Moody's old dragster which figured to be a slight bit slower than Moody's new mount. Once the final light glowed and the drivers hit the gas pedals, it seemed even more unlikely that something special might happen because Brown left first. Snively had been outfoxed at the line, but he went all out and came close to nipping Brown at the finish line. When the announcer's voice reported the times, the crowd went wild. Snively had done it, he had smashed through to the long-awaited sub–six-second run with a 5.97. But he lost the race to Brown despite the latter's higher e.t. of 6.03.

In the last pairing of Brown versus Moody, there was another treat for the fans. Brown came out too soon and redlighted. Assured of victory, Moody let 'er rip and zoomed down the Ontario asphalt to a startling 5.91 e.t.

As it happened, none of the great runs of the day brought an official record. None of the drivers backed up their low e.t.'s wih a second run within 2 percent of the first. But notice had been served, the five-second era was with us and someone would establish it officially before too long.

Recalling the memorable occasion, Terry Cook of *Hot Rod* wrote, "At first we doubted the credibility of the clocks. Ontario Motor Speedway had moved the quarter-mile drag strip about 300 feet down the front straightaway for this event [from previous years] so that the finish line coincided with the one Mario Andretti, Richard Petty, and all the other kinds of racers at OMS use. When the good times started coming over the P.A.s, everyone said that they had moved the starting line but forgot to move the finish line [thus a 1020-foot track and super-quick e.t.'s]. But the track was the right length and NHRA was running the Chrondeks. If you can't believe the times at an NHRA event, then the world is coming to an abrupt end last Wednesday. The real reason for the supertimes at the Supernats was the track surface . . . Dan Boore had coated the track surface with his VHT traction compound mix, and a heavy rain just prior to the event cleaned the unwanted elements from the asphalt. They should really have called it the Flypaper Nationals."

Though Don Moody turned his unofficial e.t. position into a recognized one in December of that year, he didn't reach the 5's. He clicked off a 6.13 performance at Long Beach, California, to close out 1972 as e.t. leader.

Everyone then looked forward to 1973 as the period when the fives would be "official." It didn't happen all at once. But the event was in the wind as drivers sniped away. In March at Gainesville, Florida, Jim Bucher lowered the NHRA official mark to 6.07 in his Chrysler rear-engine Kenner's SSP and in July, the Englishtown, New Jersey, crowd was treated to a dandy 6.03 achievement by Bill Wigginton in the Candies & Hughes Chrysler-powered digger.

Finally it happened. The first recognized sub–six-second e.t. went into the books, fittingly, at the granddaddy of all national races, the Indy Nationals. It wasn't Big Daddy Don Garlits who did it, but Gary Beck, who had the crowd buzzing for hours after he scored what amounted to a double in his rear-engine Chrysler Beck & Peets rail. Not only did he rack up a 5.96 that day in September, but simultaneously cracked the speed barrier with a 243.90 mph.

Though Don Garlits' farsighted introduction of the operational rear-engine dragster made the breakthrough possible, he had missed the cherished goal of leading everyone into the 5's. However, he made up for that oversight at the next Supernationals, bettering Beck's statistics with a 5.78 e.t. and a 247.25 mph in his Dodge-engined Wynn's Charger.

Those records were to remain untouched for almost two years. Don finally took the speed value up a few notches in Martin, Michigan, in August, 1975, hitting an official NHRA 249.30. Then in October, he hooked up with Gary Beck at the Winston World Finals for heroics in which each driver took turns for a while in keeping the record keepers spinning. During qualifying, Gary sped down the Ontario, California, track to post a world record 5.69. Gary, who had been world champion of NHRA in 1974, held the e.t. honor for only a day. Garlits capped his greatest year in his chosen field on Saturday, October 11, 1975, when he made the finals with dizzying qualifying clockings of 5.63 e.t. and 250.69 mph. He hadn't been first into the fives, but in claiming the new e.t. record, he also became the first driver in drag-racing history to smash the 250 mph barrier.

44

The next day, on his way to a victory that also gave him a slim point victory over Gary Beck for NHRA world champion, he consistently approached his qualifying e.t., zooming to an e.t. of 5.65 in one case and 5.67 in another. Many other drivers scorched the asphalt in the memorable meet. Jim Warren clocked a 5.74 in one run and, in the second round of the finals, posted the fastest losing time of 5.80 in a race won by Gary Beck.

After that wondrous day, it seemed drag racing had to sit back and take a breather for a while. Garlits' 5.63 stood alone throughout 1976 and into 1977. On the surface, it seemed to provide evidence that even the rear-engined design could only do so much for improved performance.

Gene Snow, for one, could see speeds of 300 mph and low fives ahead, but not with mid 1970s powerplants. "I think the next stop is the turbo charger. Within the next decade, we'll see another source of power replacing the internal combustion engine, something like a steam jet."

So perhaps the dragsters had hit at least a temporary limit. But then Shirley Muldowney rocketed to a new top speed of 252.10 mph in January at Phoenix, Arizona, although missing a new e.t. record. Then, in May 1977, that amazing lady topped herself at Orange County Raceway, California, with a run of 253.10 mph. Maybe, said some fans, there was life in the piston-powered digger yet. Of course, it probably wouldn't be around when—and if—the drivers got into the fours . . . or would it?

3

Big Daddy: King of 'Em All

Mention drag racing to the typical sports fan and one name comes to mind: Don "Big Daddy" Garlits. Of course, Garlits has never competed in the Funny Car or Pro Stock categories, so his name has never appeared in the winner's circle or the record book for those two top Professional brackets.

A dyed-in-the-wool hot-rodder is well aware of that as well as of the many other illustrious drivers in Don's preferred Top Fuel specialty (some of whose careers will be cited in later chapters). But in all of drag racing, few even approach the number of historic firsts achieved by Big Daddy, and almost no one has sustained excellence for over two decades as he has.

Gaining maximum acceleration, highest speed through the traps, lowest e.t.—those are the goals Garlits has always aimed for. And he has proved again and again that targets once thought impossible to reach over a quarter mile in a vehicle which begins from a standing start can be attained. Each time he lowered a barrier, he initiated a revolution in the sport. So it happened after 1964, when he shattered the long im-

With a member of his crew, super driver Don Garlits (right) pushes his finely honed racer toward the starting line for another race.

pregnable 200-mph limit, exceeding it three times in a little over a week at two different tracks. Before long, drivers across the country were being clocked at over 200 and the record steadily was raised until it went past the 250 mark in the 1970s.

If few have surpassed Big Daddy in accomplishments, fewer still in any walk of life have survived the ordeals Garlits has passed through and lived to tell the tale, much less returned to the same task and risen to new heights. Big Daddy has suffered many injuries, not the least being a dragster explosion in Chester, South Carolina, in which his body was so badly burned, doctors gave him up for dead. To their amazement, he not only fought back to health, but also licked a case of drug addiction which resulted from the massive doses of pain killers fed him during the excruciatingly painful days of his early convalescence. Later, in the early 1970s, though in his forties and past what most might consider retirement age, he came back from still another searing accident in which he lost most of his right foot. When the word "tough" was coined, it was meant to describe Big Daddy.

And yet, except for the seams and scars that mark his face and body, he hardly looks the part. He is of slight build, only a little over five feet tall and usually soft spoken. He got his nickname of Big Daddy not for his physical size, but for the amazing exploits he has performed over the years as an innovative designer/mechanic and one of the most steel-nerved competitors ever to squeeze inside the cockpit of a four-wheeled mechanical monster.

Most first-rank drivers have at least experimented with other kinds of drag vehicles. Don Prudhomme and Tom McEwen, to name two well-known experts, for years raced in both Top Fuel and Funny Car classifications. But Garlits, while he sometimes has added a Funny Car to his racing stable to be raced by another member of his team, has always remained true to the deceptively simple looking "rail," a vehicle that might be described as an engine sitting on a metal sled. As he once wrote in *Sports Illustrated,* "About those unlimited Class AA fuelers that I drive: a pure dragster is the way to get the purest acceleration and, to me, that's what the game is all about."

If Don doesn't look the part of a devil-may-care speed merchant as a man, he was even less so as a boy growing up in Tampa, Florida. Though he helped with the chores around his family's dairy farm (his father died when he was 10 and his mother ran it for a while afterward), Don's frail build and small stature made him a poor candidate for baseball, football, and the standard sports the other boys in his area preferred. He wasn't much interested in team sports. Don liked to figure things out for himself and he also had an interest in things mechanical from an early age. Automobiles fascinated him. When he reached his teens, he began to try to find out what made them tick.

As his mother told an interviewer, "When he was 14, Don erected a tripod in the backyard and pulled motors out of old cars and worked on them unceasingly. Many nights at 2 a.m., I had to force Don and his friends to quit before neighbors called police."

Don continued to tinker with cars as he went through high school, though he didn't seem to have much interest in racing them. He did well in high school, but after graduation, partly because there wasn't much money available for further education, he went to work. His first job was in a bookkeeping office. He stayed for half a year, becoming increasingly restless at the 9 to 5 routine. "I began to feel like a figure," he told a reporter. "I'd walk into the office, look around, and I'd get depressed. I thought there must be more to life than this. One day I walked in, turned around, and walked out."

He then concentrated on his first love, the automobile. He worked in various service shops before getting a job as a racing mechanic. Meanwhile, he had started to try his hand behind the wheel, racing some of his home-made hot rods on the side streets of Tampa. Storming down city streets at rates well above posted limits has never been in favor with law authorities and Garlits started having trouble with the

50

police. By nature, he wasn't a hell-raiser; he never cared for drinking. As he grew up he followed most of the tenets of the Boy Scout oath in climbing the ladder to Eagle Scout rank. (He always supported scouting. Later, when he had become one of the most famous names in the sports world, he often addressed banquets and honors nights for his own old troop and other troops in the area.)

The cars Garlits gunned through the Tampa streets were odd-looking things, stripped-down Fords with flathead engines mounted on bare frame rails or souped-up reworks of old roadsters. Those were the years of drag racing's infancy when there were no rules or regulations, even on strips set aside solely for dragging. There was little in the way of safety gear and the competitors "run what they brung." After a siege of traffic tickets and other brushes with the local gendarmes, Garlits realized he had to do something. Drag racing had become a passion with him. He married in the early 1950s and, for a while, kept his racing activities secret even from his wife.

Finally he overcame his fears of rejection from more established racers and switched his attention to the local drag strip. Once he turned his first hot rod loose on a quarter-mile length of raceway, he had found his element. His genius for coaxing every bit of efficiency possible out of reworked engines and car systems soon made him the driver to beat in Tampa. In a few years he was known as the fastest rodder in all of Florida, and other drivers were coming to him for tips on improving their own skills and equipment.

Soon his reputation spanned the continent to the cradle of organized drag racing, California. In 1955, Garlits was included in the "Drag Safari" arranged by officials of the National Hot Rod Association to popularize regulated, law-abiding drag racing with enthusiasts from coast to coast. During the tour, Garlits opened some eyes with a Top Eliminator win in which he achieved the then amazing e.t. of 12.5 seconds.

Even those who saw it thought it might be a one-time fluke. Few expected an upstart young racer from the remote strips of Florida driving home-made racers would continue to seriously threaten the reigning champs of the California circuit whose costlier, more sophisticated vehicles regularly set new world speed records. Indeed, though Don won steadily in his home region the next year or two, little attention was paid to him up to the time he traveled northward in 1957 to enter the World Series of Drag Racing at Cordova, Illinois.

The big favorite was the dragster of the Cook & Bedwell team, driven by the well-regarded Emery Cook. In a period when most racers were happy to edge into the 150 mph range, the Cook & Bedwell digger exceeded 160 mph time after time. So no one paid much attention to the somewhat ungainly four wheeler piloted by Garlits when it was paired with the West Coast speedster. To the amazement of the audience and the drag experts, once the starter's flag came down, the "kid" from Florida roared out in front and stayed there down through the finish line.

But those years weren't unbroken times of glory. Don lost plenty of races and added lines of worry to his mother's face with both minor and serious injuries. In one mishap he was badly burned in a fire that kept him wrapped in bandages for many days and brought his weight down to a frightening 85 pounds. As always, Don shrugged off the dangers and returned to racing as soon as he was fit again. As the decade moved to a close he felt the time was at hand to invade the citadel of racing and prove to Californians once and for all that he was a force to be reckoned with.

Word of some of his feats had reached the coast by then. He had raised eyebrows two years earlier, in 1957, when he cracked the supposedly unbreakable 170-mph barrier to achieve a new world's record of 176.45 mph. There were plenty of California drag enthusiasts who had doubts about that. After all, technical experts had worked up extensive calculations to prove a drag racer, even the most advanced, couldn't develop the required acceleration over only 1,320 feet to go

Flames from the rear engine exhaust pipes cast eerie shadows over Don Garlits' helmeted, fireproof-suited figure as he prepares to prove again he's the king of top fuel racing.

175 or 180 mph through the traps. And when they looked at pictures of the car this eastern upstart supposedly used to shatter all those theories, the possibility seemed even less likely. The car had relatively bulky wheels and tires up front, obviously didn't have a lightweight chassis and was powered by an unsupercharged engine.

Knowledgeable fans, not only in California but in other hotbeds of racing activity, suggested there might have been an error. Perhaps, they conjectured, the timing systems at the tracks Garlits ran weren't accurate enough. Or perhaps some of his superspeed runs were flukes that couldn't be repeated during major race events. And anyway, even if Garlits did turn some surprising speeds on occasion, had he proved himself against all comers in the very best competition available?

In fact, argued some Californians, why didn't he come west to show what he was made of? Why did 1957 and all of 1958 go by without a visit to drag strips in Southern California or Bakersfield from this new claimant to drag-racing royalty? When word came in 1959 that the Florida flash was finally going to show up at Bakersfield, many of his detractors gleefully lay in wait for his debut there.

When he moved into the starting lane in a dragster that looked just as ungainly as the pictures of his 1957 car, the audience really whooped it up. Jeers and catcalls rained down as well as occasional beer cans and other objects. "Look at that," said some. "With that junk heap, his name must be Don Garbage, not Don Garlits!" Cries of "Tampa Don" and "swamp rat" also poured forth.

But Don went about his business and paid little outward attention to the crowd. In fact, the roar and vibration of his engine easily drowned out the heckling. Besides, Garlits was sure he had the answer to that: proof that his claims to excellence were true. He knew as well that he had a secret weapon circulating through the carburetor and cylinders of his carefully nurtured powerplant. For Garlits, then as in years since, was a master at blending fuel to get the maximum amount of horsepower from the engine through the transmission and down to the wheels. That was

54

what had propelled his racer to phenomenal speeds even though the hot rod itself, in traditional fashion, was built to a great extent from reclaimed junkyard parts.

Once Garlits started to smoke his way down the track, the sneers and catcalls faded away. From then on people in ever increasing numbers came not to jeer but to marvel at the accomplishments of the compact Floridian. Garlits made one of the Bakersfield taunts a mark of honor by naming most of his racers after that time "Swamp Rat." And each new Swamp Rat model that rolled out of the Don Garlits Speed Shop back home featured some innovation which upgraded drag-racing technology one more notch.

In the early 1960s Garlits' rising popularity made him a major drawing card at tracks across the United States. He won a good share of events, though it took several years before his name started appearing as overall victor in what are considered the major championships of the main hot-rod associations. One reason is that there weren't many such races sanctioned in the early 1960s. The "daddy of 'em all," the National Hot Rod Association's Nationals, which eventually settled in Indianapolis, remained the only such event sanctioned by NHRA from the first meet in 1955 until 1961 when NHRA added a second National Championship competition, the Winternationals. Those remained NHRA's only two national races until 1965.

As the 1960s began, it appeared certain to observers that it was only a matter of time until Garlits became the national top-fuel king. He was running well and coming up with innovations such as wire wheels and frame improvements that started new trends in the field. The result was a rapid lowering of e.t.'s and raising of top speeds until everyone began talking about the possibility of cracking 200 mph sometime within the decade.

Then, just when things seemed brightest for him, disaster struck. At the time safety suits and special safety equipment had not become standard in the sport. Without those aids, Garlits was so badly injured

55

in an accident on the Chester, South Carolina, track that doctors thought he might not live, much less come back to race again.

He told Mark Kram of *Sports Illustrated,* "The supercharger exploded and only my leather jacket saved me. It all happened in four seconds. I had swallowed some of the fire and later I caught pneumonia. My condition was similar to that of Fireball Roberts who died this year. [Roberts was a famous stock car driver.] I had third degree burns; flesh, especially on my hands, was just hanging off."

During the ordeal Garlits remembers the way the face of a doctor seemed to float into view. The man's words were terrifying: "My God! We can't do anything for this man."

Despite it all, Garlits' strong constitution and unbending will to live triumphed. Through months of treatment and long drawn out hours of pain his spirit remained firm. He overcame the burns, beat off pneumonia, and finally was on the way to recovery from the injuries inflicted by the explosion.

That, however, was only half of it. Garlits suddenly came face to face with an even more implacable enemy that resulted from the accident: drug addiction.

He recalled to Kram, "One of the worst things about the accident was the convalescence. They had socked a lot of morphine into me to kill the pain; in fact, I used to count the minutes waiting for the shots. Well, when I went home, I was hooked on the stuff. I could never sleep and then there was this terrible gnawing inside. For days I had to go for long walks. I used to walk until 4 o'clock in the morning, until I was too tired to walk anymore. I kicked it eventually, but it was one of the worst trials of my life. When I was burned again, not as seriously, I wouldn't take any of that stuff. The whole thing was a nightmare. . . . I still dream about it now and then—those four seconds that seemed like four years."

Still, Garlits would not give up racing, despite the pleadings of family and friends. Once he was mended, he went back behind the wheel of his beloved Swamp Rats. For a while, he admits, the fear held sway.

56

Sometimes he found it hard to get his foot to obey and press the gas pedal "down to the wood."

Many thought Garlits' days in racing were numbered, that he would have to retire. Few expected he would return to his old form, let alone set new marks. But they didn't know their man. In 1964 Garlits was running as well as ever, and he suddenly sent shock waves through the drag-racing field in August, 1964, when he rocketed down the strip at a Detroit track to establish the first recognized 200-mph plus time. (Some drivers had claimed going over 200 mph previously, but those were at small tracks where the timing system was not considered up to the standards of the major sanctioning bodies.)

Some racing authorities even had reservations about the Detroit run, noting that Garlits had gone over 200 mph only once that day and then only by a hair. The very next week, Big Daddy took his Wynn's Jammer digger to Great Meadows, New Jersey, for an AHRA meet and chalked up over 200 mph in back-to-back runs, in one of which he easily eliminated his longtime rival, Chris (The Greek) Karamesines. His top speed of the day was well past the 200-mph barrier—201.34.

Soon after, Big Daddy was encamped in Indianapolis, waiting for a chance to take the superbowl of drag racing, the NHRA Nationals. Unlike the early days in California, the only shouts Garlits heard at Indy were roars of encouragement. Much of the huge gathering had come out primarily to see the man who had shattered almost every record of importance in top-fuel racing. He only needed a win at Indy to cement his claim to being the king of drag racing. It was an impressive field of course, the winningest, fastest drivers the sport could produce. But it was Garlits' year and he swept on to victory in the sudden-death competition in race after race. When the smoke had cleared in the finals, Don had his first major championship and was to come back twice more before the 1960s were over—in 1967 and 1968—to claim the crown of the Nationals.

Throughout the 1960s Don showed up at almost every major race

Big Daddy whips through the speed traps at Ontario Motor Speedway in October, 1975, to become the first drag racer ever to crack the 250-mph barrier.

of both the NHRA and the AHRA. In most years he walked off with firsts in one or more major competitions of each group. Thus he didn't take the NHRA Nationals in 1966, but smashed all existing speed records that year by winning the AHRA Nationals with a low e.t. of 7.77 and 219.55 mph. (Don always remained active in AHRA ranks, a group he had helped found and which he served as president from 1956 until his disastrous accident of 1960).

Unusual occurrences repeatedly dotted his career. As an example, in 1965, he ended up, in effect, racing himself at the Bakersfield fuel and gas championships. He brought two top-fuel dragsters and his team included another expert driver, Marvin Schwartz. He made the finals with his first day performance in his Wynn's Jammer. Not wanting to sit around while the other top drivers worked their way through the eliminations to choose the other finalist, he took Schwartz's usual mount, the Garlits Chassis Special and reentered the lists. Setting a blistering pace, he turned back one famous driver after another until he had placed the second vehicle in the runoff. So the last race pitted Garlits in the Jammer against Schwartz in the alternate digger. It was no contest; Don ripped down the course to hit the lights well ahead of Marvin, bringing the crowd to its feet as the announcer reported the 205 mph mark.

When the 1960s drew to a close, it was hard to find much more Don could accomplish. He was the most feared driver in the most competitive bracket in all of drag racing and had been national champ of AHRA and in the national top 10 of NHRA many times. Few major crowns had eluded him over the years. But he was pushing forty, and plenty of young, talented drivers were pointing for him at every meet— superstars or potential superstars like Don Prudhomme, Danny Ongais, and John Wiebe. While Garlits had earlier retired briefly several times, he never stayed on the sidelines more than the time needed to recover from injuries. Now, however, many thought he should step aside permanently. He was at the peak of his skills and had done so much for the sport, no one wanted him to suffer the indignity of becoming an also-ran or hazard another, perhaps fatal, crash.

Then it seemed lady luck might take a hand in the matter. In 1969 Don broke an ankle in a motorcycle accident and missed many races. He ignored suggestions he use that as an excuse for quitting. When the 1970 season began, Garlits put his equipment on the truck and started his usual trek around the nation. One of his goals was the AHRA Grand American Championship at Lions Drag Strip in Southern California. The crowds were large and boisterous and particularly pleased to see the most luminous driver in the sport in action. Don responded with some fine runs that moved him into the final rounds.

On March 8 he moved his dragster into position for an elimination run and began his preparations. The staccato burst of the engine and the swirling smoke were watched with excited anticipation by everyone in the stands and along the rail when suddenly there was a louder, more penetrating noise. The vehicle seemed to disintegrate before everyone's eyes. The two-speed transmission (another Garlits achievement was perfection of a two-speed drive system for dragsters) had shaken apart and the explosion shattered the car and blasted away most of Don's right foot. As the ambulance sped Garlits to the hospital, onlookers sadly decided the great career of the Swamp Rat was finally over.

Garlits, however, demonstrated again that his career was akin to the cat with nine lives. He recovered rapidly and, using a special padded shoe on his mangled right foot, was back on the top-fuel circuit in three months. He ran reasonably well, too, winning some races and always remaining in contention in others. In the back of his mind he was making plans for a new revolution in dragster design that would greatly reduce the likelihood of serious accidents like the one that had recently hit him.

He got his racing team together in his shop in Seffner, Florida, and calmly informed them that the next step was to develop a rear-engined dragster. Having the engine behind the driver provided better vision, but more important, it meant that flying metal or leaking fuel during a run would go back onto the track, not into the driver's face. Other people had attempted to develop rear-engine systems without success. The consensus was it couldn't be done. But Garlits had heard that refrain before. Settling down to work, Garlits and his associates put their tremendous experience to work to carefully figure out the proper combination of weight distribution and aerodynamic surfaces. As the time for the kickoff NHRA race of the 1971 season, the Winternationals in Pomona, California, came closer, Garlits was sure he had the problem solved.

Even so, many heads shook when he moved his rear-engine digger from the pits to the starting line the first time. It didn't take long for Don to prove his point. He qualified with a good 6.84 e.t., roughly in the middle of a spread by other entrants from a low of 6.70 to a high of 7.03. He romped to victory in his first Top Fuel Eliminator run with a 6.85 win over Tommy Allen. He followed with impressive victories over John Nichols and Carl Olson, hitting 6.70 e.t. each time and a 6.70 semifinal triumph over John Dunn. Only the formidable Kenny Safford barred the way to another striking chapter in the Garlits saga. That threat quickly evaporated when damage suffered by the Safford car in the semifinals couldn't be repaired in time for the finals. Garlits made a solo victory run, thrilling the crowd by smoking his tires all the way down the strip.

A new era had begun. By proving the rear-engine car could work, Garlits helped fight off the growing challenge to Top Fuel drag supremacy by the upstart Funny Cars. The new design flexibility the arrangement provided gave racers the chance to sharply cut the e.t.'s so that the rising Funny Car marks couldn't bring that class to the eminence of fastest in the world. In 1970 and 1971, driving in the high sixes had become fairly common for top Funnies, but Garlits' breakthrough brought the opportunity for Top Fuelers to run in the mid and even low sixes. Don demonstrated that admirably at the NHRA Springnationals when he turned an eye-popping 6.44 seconds and 227.27 mph on one run. A little later in 1971, he set drag racing on its ear again at his home track in Gainesville, Florida, blazing to a win with a then astounding 6.26 e.t.

The rear-engine concept turned 1971 into one of Garlits' best years ever, a surprising turn of events for a man many thought was overripe for the rocking chair. He annexed the championship of the AHRA by taking the World Finals at Fremont, California, then set his cap for an unprecedented double if he could take the Indy Nationals. He started out at Indy as though he would do just that, blazing down the strip the first day of qualifying with a seemingly effortless 6.21 e.t. He figured it would psych out most of the others, and to a great extent it did. Even such a normally cool racer as Don Prudhomme felt the pressure and was sent to the trailer in the first round.

As the preliminaries went by, no one could come close to Don's 6.21. Meanwhile, he zoomed past every opponent to make the finals and a chance to become the first driver in history to win the Nationals four times. His rival was Steve Carbone, in a Chrysler hemi-powered front-engine dragster, one of the few who kept his head about Garlits' achievement. Carbone knew he couldn't match the rear-engined machine head on; he needed strategy to win. The resulting race remains one of the classics fans still talk about.

When the two dragsters were moved into the staging lane, Garlits stalked up to Carbone and told him, "You will stage first in the final round." To which Carbone responded, "Don't bet on it, old man." Garlits had made the first move in the chess game and Carbone had countered. Now came the real test.

In its 1972 Yearbook, a reporter for *Popular Hot Rodding* recalled the scene: "Both cars pushed down and fired, took one burnout in the bleach box and lit the 'pre-stage' light on the Christmas Tree. And then both cars just sat there. And sat there. And sat there. Garlits winged his motor. Carbone winged back at him. It was a classic confrontation and it cost Garlits the race. For almost two minutes the cars sat in the pre-stage beams, neither moving. Finally, after some frantic appeals from [the starter], Big Daddy staged, followed immediately by Carbone. Then there was the green light and Carbone was gone, while Garlits went up in smoke on the starting line. Steve streaked to a 6.48 second e.t. at 229.00 mph and Don recovered to post a 6.65, 229.00 run in a valiant losing effort."

There was no doubt the better car had lost. Had Garlits staged right away, his engine was hot and ready to go while his opponent's was still cold and sputtering. The delay made Garlits' engine overheat and permitted Carbone's to get to proper running temperature. But even though Big Daddy lost, the race remains one of the greatest in drag history. And it certainly was only a prelude to further Garlits' achievements in later years. (In 1975, Garlits finally claimed his fourth Indy Nationals win.)

His rear-engine idea quickly became the rule for the field. From 1972 on, a front-engine vehicle became a rarity and the speeds and e.t.'s rapidly moved to new records. Though Don dominated drag racing in 1971, thanks to the rear-engine edge, once he opened the door to new innovations the many other highly skilled racing teams were quick to catch up. So much so that Don essentially was shutout of the major winner's circles in 1972. Still, no one could deny the importance of his rear-engine move, perhaps the greatest achievement of his long and eventful career.

Don was not through yet. He refined his digger still more in the off season, worked a little more magic in his fuel alchemy and started 1973 in glory with a win at Pomona, the third time he made the Winternationals laurels his own. He closed out the season with a second major NHRA triumph, capturing the Supernationals at Ontario Race Track, California, with a top speed of 244.56 mph and an e.t. of 5.78. In between, another e.t. milestone fell, the fives—that is, e.t.'s under the 6.00 second level—though not to Garlits. The breakthrough, though, was to a rear-engined car (the race is detailed in Chapter 2), and the winner of every major NHRA Top Fuel competition was a rear-engine car.

There were still more pinnacles for Garlits to scale as the 1970s progressed. In 1975, he started out with a fourth victory at the Winternationals. As the season went by, he engaged in a nip-and-tuck battle with Canadian ace Gary Beck for the NHRA TFE driver's championship. When they both appeared for the final NHRA race meet at Ontario in October he trailed Beck by 148 points 8,227 to 8,375.

After coming from obscurity a few years earlier, Beck had gained many fans, so there was plenty of cheering for his efforts. But Garlits, as always, was the supreme competitor. On Saturday, he took his rear-engined Keith Black powered four wheeler to the staging line, took the green and shot straight as an arrow down the asphalt. The onlookers gasped in amazement when the times were announced—an unbelievable 5.63 second e.t. and a speed of 250.69 mph, both world's records that stood into 1977 when Shirley Muldowney took over top speed honors.

The pressure was too much for Beck, who was turned aside in the preliminaries on Sunday, October 12. Garlits swept through to the finals where he faced the formidable Herman Peterson. But he blew down Peterson's challenge with a fine showing of 5.74 e.t. and 247.93 mph. When the smoke had cleared and the points added up, Garlits had snaked past Beck, 9,693 points to 8,990. In all his glorious career Don had not been able to be overall NHRA world champion, though he'd come close several times. In the wake of his sweetest win, he announced he would retire. "That's it, that's my last big race. You can't race forever. I put 25 years into it and this is a perfect time to quit. I'm out of drag racing completely."

Don Prudhomme protested, "Old man, you've got to be kidding, you can't quit. You're just learning how to drive."

And, like Muhammad Ali, Garlits showed a champion can change his mind. He didn't race in NHRA in 1976, it's true, but he competed in AHRA events and in 1977 once more was represented in races sponsored by all major sanctioning groups. His 1977 achievements included winning the IHRA championship, finishing in the top 10 in NHRA point standings and taking on '77 NHRA champion Shirley Muldowney in a series of match races.

The thrill of competing was like life's blood to Don, as he told one reporter who asked him how long Big Daddy meant to keep racing: "I'll race as long as it's fun, because that's what it's supposed to be. If the sanctioning bodies make it too much of a hassle or my health gives up, then I think I'll quit. I just like to race and although I make a lot of money, that's not the point. I can make money many other ways."

4

The Family That Drag Races Together

One of the memorable moments in ABC's Wide World of Sports took place in late January, 1970. It occurred during the closing minutes of coverage of the Winternationals from Pomona, California, when the camera focused on a small boy sitting on the lap of the driver of the winning Top Fuel AA dragster. The sun was going down and the four-year-old had a winsome smile as he put up his fingers in a victory sign. Behind the dragster was the push car, driven by a good looking blonde woman whose face also glowed with enthusiasm and pride.

The driver was young Larry Dixon, Sr., the small boy his son Larry, Jr., and the young woman Pat Dixon, wife and mother. In the mid 1970s, by then augmented by a daughter, the Dixons remained a close-knit family, devoted to each other and to drag racing. Even before he was high school age, Larry, Jr., was a regular crew member, helping pour the burnout compounds around the wheels of his father's dragster. He also helped direct the car into position in the staging lanes.

The Dixons symbolized the sport of drag racing in several ways. By the 1970s it had long gotten away from its early image of rowdiness and

The drag racing Dixons: Larry, Sr., holding his young daughter; Pat Dixon; Larry, Jr.

a male "Macho" approach. From the late 1950s on, it had become a family event, both for the drivers, many of whom took wives and children along to races and on tour, and for the audiences. At any strip it's common to see parents and grandparents as well as children of all ages sharing picnic lunches in the stands or wandering past the frenzied activity in the pits.

But the Dixons also stand for another aspect of drag racing: the original do-it-yourself idea. Just as thousands of amateur racers saved their money to buy parts and do work in their spare time, so did Larry and Pat Dixon keep their top-fuel dragster operation a backyard hobby. Both of them earned salaries from either full-time or part-time jobs to help pay for fuel, parts, and the many other expenses of keeping a racing car going.

When you pull into the driveway of the Dixon home in the San Fernando Valley section of Los Angeles, you first see a sign advertising the Lollipop Day School. Pat runs the school, taking care of small children in the enclosed backyard and the back-of-the-house playroom. While she does this, Larry may be off from his regular job and working on the dragster which occupies the garage or perhaps storing supplies in the trailer-truck that carries the dragster from one drag strip to another. Pat earns money in other ways as well. One activity is raising Chinchilla Persian cats. Sometimes she works nights or part-time days as a secretary or file clerk.

Larry usually works as a skilled mechanic for an automotive concern. There are many people who own companies associated either with racing or in specialized car areas, such as sports cars, who take an interest in racing and racers. So, as Larry says, "The man I work for lets me take off the time I need to go racing and also lets me use the company's tools and equipment. Of course, I still have to pay my way. I may have to work nights to make it up. I don't like to do it too much; I like to come home and be with my family at night."

Pat, says Larry, doesn't gripe about his going off to races. For one thing, she loves the idea of his racing and always wants to go along to watch and help out. Nor does she object to her children following in their parent's footsteps.

"We always arrange things so the kids can go away with us to almost all the races," she says. "It's a family situation. When our second child was due several years ago I went along with Larry to one race in mid May just before I gave birth. We got back from the race and on Tuesday I went into the hospital and had a girl. I got out of the hospital in a few days, in time to accompany Larry to a meet in Bakersfield, California. Our daughter was four days old when she attended her first drag race. People who knew us were shocked to see me pregnant one weekend and slimmed down with a very pretty daughter in my arms the next."

And yet Pat Dixon has no desire to get behind the wheel of a racing car herself. "I have no interest whatsoever in drag racing for myself. High speeds scare me. If Larry goes over 55 miles per hour on the freeway, I get uptight. But I feel good about Larry's racing. I have no fear at all about him driving top-fuel dragsters. Funny Cars are something else. I don't like to think about a driver being cooped up in those tight plastic bodies when fumes or flames get into the cockpit. I like the idea of Larry driving top fuelers. I want him out in the open like that."

For Larry a love affair with automobiles started early in life. Along with that came a feeling of pleasure about working with his hands. "My dad was a craftsman, so I've always been around mechanics. He was an auto mechanic at first and later worked as a machinist for an aircraft company. When I became interested in cars, he showed me how they worked and later helped me build some of my early racers."

Larry's introduction to drag racing came somewhat accidentally in the mid 1950s. "I had a steady girl at the time, and when she went away on vacation, I didn't know what to do with myself. I went to the local San Fernando Drag Strip (no longer in existence) and on the spur

70

of the moment competed with my little two barrel Chevy. I lucked out and won a trophy and that started it all."

After that, Larry began spending time with some friends who had Corvette engines in souped-up sedans. "So I worked at jobs and saved money until I could buy my own Corvette to put in a 1955 Bel-Air Chevy. My dad helped out. He ran me around to shops to get head work done, engines bored, and so on."

That was the first of seven 1955 Chevy versions Larry built, each a bit flashier and faster than the last. At first he tried street racing with friends. But after he got a number of expensive tickets from the gendarmes, he decided that was not the way to go. He switched his attention to the drag strips, one of his steps being to go to a 1958 Corvette engine with supercharging which let him exceed 140 mph over the quarter mile on a number of occasions.

For a time, Larry took his engine and switched to a 1941 Willys Coupe. "It was plenty ugly, but it ran pretty well. For a while, I ran it with a stickshift. I finally put a B & M Hydromatic in, but with a small Chevy engine, it still wouldn't keep up with Chrysler-engined cars."

Dixon's reputation as a driver was steadily building in Southern California as the 1950s went by. This led to his getting a driving assignment for a while from fuel dragster owner Jack Bynum who had a chassis, but no engine. Larry supplied the engine and had his first taste of top-fuel eliminator competition.

Larry moved back to the sportsman class after one season with the Bynum and Dixon fueler. He combined forces with a muffler shop owner named Al Voges who had a promising 1948 Fiat body that seemed well suited for Class AA/Fuel Altereds. Larry installed his 1,000 hp Chevy engine and spent long hours getting the supercharger to work properly. Finally he decided the car was ready for some all-out racing. He took it out to the San Fernando strip for what was to prove one of the more trying days of his career.

First he ran into problems from fumes. "The car was running well,

Larry, Jr., at left, helps his father complete a burnout maneuver at the NHRA Nationals.

but we hadn't realized there was an opening into the cockpit section in the rear wheel wells. We smoked the tires and the cockpit filled with it and with a plexiglass windshield the air didn't circulate to clear the smoke."

But worse was to come. After closing off the opening, Larry started another run and got the Fiat moving down the strip at close to 150 mph. Larry wanted to slow down, but when he tried to lift the throttle, it was stuck. The car began to cartwheel and all he could do was stay put and hope for the best. "The car kept rolling and rolling and I lost count. Everything was a blur and I remember wondering is it ever going to stop? It seemed like I went over around 50 times, but later when I saw a film of it, it was only seven times." Dixon walked away from the spectacular crash dazed, but unhurt. The Fiat was a pile of junk, but the engine was still in fairly good condition.

So Larry took his trusty powerplant and started over again, this time building a competition roadster that was sponsored by a restaurant called the Fireside Inn. The Model-T Ford with its "Mickey Mouse" plastic roadster body became the terror of the Competition Eliminator Class. Dixon's fuel-burning vehicle regularly hit 200 mph and, particularly after he switched from the Chevy engine to an early 392 cubic inch Chrysler, it became a threat to top-fuel dragsters. During those years, the mid 1960s, Dixon, cheered on by Pat, whom he met and married in 1966, often challenged and defeated Top Fuelers at such local tracks as Lions, Irwindale, and Orange County.

The car worked too well. Many drivers complained it represented unfair competition. The sanctioning bodies eventually responded by eliminating fuel-burning "modified roadsters" from drag-racing categories and Larry and Pat had to look for some other way of staying in the sport they loved so much.

"There wasn't much we could do with the old car then. Since the roadster was built to be a roadster, when you took the body off there was nothing there for other classes of drag racing. It looked as if our best bet was to sell the roadster and try to find a way to get another kind of racing car."

As luck would have it, the opportunity to change directions was dropped in their laps almost immediately. A man named Darrell Greenemeyer built a top-fuel car with Smirnoff Vodka as a sponsor. At first, he decided to try driving it himself, but that didn't work out too well. "The man who built the engine for him," Dixon recalls, "was my engine man, Dave Zuchel, and when Greenemeyer told him he wanted to have someone else drive, he thought of me. One day he saw me and asked if I was tired of driving a roadster. He suggested I get together with Greenemeyer and see if we could work things out.

"Actually, I'd heard Smirnoff's was looking for a driver, but I didn't think about applying to operate a supercar like that. Knowing Zuchel would put in a word for me made it seem different. I went down to the shop one time and Greenemeyer asked me to try it out. But he's smaller than I am and when I tried to climb into the cockpit, I kicked out the windshield. When I got squeezed in, I had to slump forward to keep my head below the roll bar, which was really low. When I got out, I said I wanted to try driving the car, but with those problems, I figured they wouldn't want me.

"So I was really surprised when Greenemeyer called up two or three days later and said to come on down. I was in heaven, because I'd never been in super Top Fuel racing before and I'd always dreamt of someday doing it."

Soon after, the car was scheduled to compete in a meet at Irwindale. Excitement ran high in the Dixon household and Larry and Pat could hardly wait for the chance to get the truck with the dragster out to the track. However, even though the team was on the road before the sun rose, the traffic was much slower near the track than expected. At 5, the time when qualification was officially closed for the event, the Smirnoff caravan still hadn't gotten to the pits.

Larry recalls, "We got there at 5:30. We couldn't compete, but I decided to make a run anyway. I just wanted to see if I could drive top fuel. Well, I let 'er rip and we set the low e.t., so I knew I was on my way."

Larry proved it to other drag enthusiasts the very next race, which was the 1967 P.D.A. at Long Beach. He had some anxious moments during qualifying when he hit an oil slick three-quarters of the way down the strip and had to lift the throttle. Despite that, the car qualified and Larry's first-round pairing was Jerry Ruth, one of the most highly regarded young drivers. Hailing from Seattle, Washington, Ruth had been the NHRA Northwest Divisional Champion in Top Fuel the two preceding years. Jerry taught Larry some of the tricks of the trade.

"Ruth and I got together to flip a coin to see who'd get to choose the lane. I'd never talked to a name driver before and I was a little nervous. He didn't say much. I remember he looked me up and down and said, 'So you're Larry Dixon.' I thought my pants weren't zipped up. I realized later it was one way a veteran racer tried to shake a newcomer up a little."

But Larry withstood the psyching. "At Long Beach in 1967 there was just one amber before the green. All tracks do that now, but at that time most used the full Tree. I'd been running there and he probably wasn't familiar with the track. As soon as I saw the yellow, I left, but he stood there for a split second. We both set low e.t. for the meet—7.02 seconds—but I eliminated him. Unfortunately, I melted a piston on the run and had to thrash to put it together. When we went up for the next round, we sprang a leak so we shut down.

"For a long time after that, I seemed to have the Indian sign on Ruth. I raced him with another car (the Howard Cam Rattler) and every time we met, I beat him. But I got to know Jerry better and found he's just a super guy. Of course, he finally did beat me, which probably helped our friendship."

Dixon raced the Smirnoff car for several more months in 1967, but Zuchel found it difficult to find the time to work on the engine. "So the car went downhill. Greenemeyer decided to take over as driver again, but he couldn't do any better than he had before. He put the car in the hangar and I think it's been there ever since."

Now that Larry and Pat had had a taste of top-fuel racing, they knew that was where they wanted to stay. The next year, he got a pledge of support from the Howard Cam Company. The result was a mean-looking contender called the Howard Cam Rattler which Larry unveiled for the 1969 season.

In a short time, he proved he could run with the big boys in the most prestigious category of drag racing. He piloted the Howard Cam Rattler to two important victories within a few month's time. One was a first at the 1969 PDA Championships at Orange County Raceway and the other a triumph at the 1969 Hot Rod Magazine Championships at Riverside Raceway near San Bernardino, California. (The event proved to be the last drag race held at that famous road racing facility). Larry didn't end up in the money at any of the major NHRA or AHRA national meets, but he won several other small competitions, including the Orange County Nitro Championships.

He now set his sights on bigger game. "With the money we won during the 1969 season, we decided to run on our own again and we built ourselves a new top fueler." The very first time in competition, the front-engine slingshot dragster brought Dixon the national renown which came with his televised Winternationals victory. That upset win over the most famous names in drag racing brought Larry the respect of his peers as a first-rank driver. However, one win doesn't make a career and it's difficult to maintain momentum when you're a self-financed driver competing against teams sponsored by major companies or wealthy sportsmen.

Not that Larry or Pat worried too much about it. They were doing what they liked and doing reasonably well at it. But the same car that won the Winternationals almost brought tragedy to the Dixons. Larry recalls, "It happened when we blew the engine in the lights in 1971 at

Lions Drag Strip in Long Beach, California. The explosion blew the crankshaft rods and pistons out the bottom of the car. I hardly had a chance to respond when the vibration shook the fire extinguisher loose in the cockpit and it knocked me out. I was unconscious the whole while the car bounced and rolled across the asphalt with flames coming from the engine."

Pat was watching from the sidelines when it happened and fought to hold down a sickening feeling. "Watching it, you couldn't tell what was going on. All you could see was a ball of fire as the car bounced over the guard rail and then back onto the track again. I got into the push car and hit the pedal to the floor. I beat the ambulance down there. As I came up, people rushed over and tried to get me to stay away. 'He's dead, stay away, he's dead,' they cried.

"But I couldn't believe that about Larry. I fought my way to where he was. He was in shock, but he was still breathing. They put him in the ambulance and I sat there by his side. As we sped to the hospital with the siren screaming, he regained consciousness. He looked at me and wanted to know if he could build another race car. I said 'sure.'"

It turned out that Larry not only was very much alive, but actually suffered few injuries other than some burns on his face and legs. Even those were minor, and Larry stayed in the hospital for only three days. He came home with bandages on his legs and some across his face covering his eyes, but in a few weeks he had them off and was eagerly making plans with Pat for a new dragster.

It was the spring of 1971 and all drag racing was agog about the new rear-engine revolution started by Don Garlits. "Everyone was changing to rear-engine designs, but Pat and I had our doubts about how safe it really was, so we built another front-engine car. It ran fairly good and we made a little money, but it soon became obvious it was hard to keep up with the top racers without a rear engine."

So when a friend offered to build a rear-engine car for the 1972 season, the Dixons went along with the idea. Larry was working for Ed

77

Pink Racing Engines at the time, so he decided to use one of the late model 426 hemi-engines Pink was famous for. But most people who use the finely tuned engines made by Pink, Keith Black Racing Engines, and the other top powerplant makers have big budgets that can take care of the cost of replacement parts if something goes wrong.

Pat points out, "The 426 was much more expensive to buy than what we were used to and if something broke and you didn't have winnings to help pay for new parts, you were in trouble. Well, we ran into a bad streak when we took our rear-engine car into the field. We weren't able to get qualifying money in most cases and we blew up one engine and then ruined its replacement."

"We decided that wasn't the way to go for us," Larry says ruefully. "Howard Cam's owner, Jerry Johansen, was still a friend and Jerry still wanted to work with us. The company suggested it would build a new car with an improved Chevy engine. I kinda' laughed, because in the 1970s, it seemed silly to try to buck the Chryslers and Dodges with a Chevy engine. But he was working with a driver named Jim Bucher who was doing very well with a Chevy and he told me what Bucher was accomplishing. So I agreed and we put an engine together and got the car ready."

The powerplant was a Chevrolet "rat" motor, so the new dragster bore the name Howard Cam Rat among the lettered items on the body. Meanwhile, Jim Bucher continued to show that a Chevy car could be competitive. In March of that year (1973), he took his Kenner's SSP down the asphalt at Gainesville, Florida, in an e.t. of 6.07, whch set a new NHRA record that lasted for four months until Bill Wigginton erased the mark with a swift 6.03 in his Chrysler-powered Candies & Hughes digger at Englishtown, New Jersey.

Dixon felt comfortable enough behind the wheel of his new car and got some reasonably good performances from it. He didn't win any major races, but he did place well in some minor races and take prize money here and there in bigger events. With Pat's usual frugal managing and budgeting, it was enough to keep things going. As she notes, "We never had to worry much about getting rich. But most of the time Larry had done well enough to make the car pay for itself. We usually figure that the money you get for qualifying at important races will pay our expenses."

The year 1973 went by in that fashion, at least for most of the time up to the final NHRA natonal championship series of the year, the Supernationals at Ontario Motor Speedway. The Dixons and Jerry Johansen brought the dragster out to the track early in the morning on qualifying day with hopes for a good result, but not expecting anything very unusual. With opponents like Gary Beck, who'd set the first official sub–six-second e.t. in NHRA two months earlier in a Chrysler-powered car, and the ever-dominant Big Daddy Garlits with his Dodge rear-engine job, a front-engine Chevy didn't figure to do anything too sensational.

But Larry, with Larry, Jr., lending encouragement and Jerry Johansen helping in the pits, tuned up everything in the Cam Rat as precisely as possible and determined to do his best. And his best turned out to be unusually good. On one run, he shot out of the staging lane in perfect unison with the shift from amber to green on the Christmas Tree and guided the car down the super-fast Ontario track without any waste motion. By the time the parachute blossomed at the far end of the course, Pat and his other rooters had a feeling he'd done something out of the ordinary. And it soon was verified: the Howard Cam Rat had swept down the quarter mile in an elapsed time of 5.94 seconds.

It was the best any Chevrolet-powered dragster had ever run and the first time a Chevy had cracked into the fives. Cragar Industries had formed a Five-Second Club in 1972, originally for the first 8 drivers to dip beneath six seconds e.t. and later expanded to 16. With his feat, Larry Dixon became the seventh driver to join the exclusive fraternity which included such other luminaries as Don Garlits, Gary Beck, Don Moody, TV Tommy Ivo, the late Mike Snively, and James Warren.

Larry received a treasured five-second jacket and an artist's portrait commemorating the occasion. The portrait now hangs proudly on his living room wall in North Hollywood.

"It was one of my greatest thrills," he agrees. "But it was tough on Jim Bucher. He'd been running a Chevy well for so long and we beat him into the Cragar Club." (Later Bucher had his day in the sun with some great seasons with a rear-engine Chevy. In 1975, he became the only driver of a Chevy-powered car to win a NHRA national event when he captured first place at the 1975 Summernationals. That same year, he also took over the title of "World's fastest Chevy" from Dixon when he sat a mark of 5.91 during qualifying for the Winston World Finals.)

Larry got to the second round of the finals at Ontario in 1973. "But then I smoked the tires and vibrated coming out of the chute and I got off the throttle. But it had been a great few days for us and I couldn't complain too much."

The story since then has been a familiar one for drivers without massive sponsor support. The Dixons continue to do well enough to keep going without the chance for any sustained run at the grand prizes.

"We haven't won any big events with the Chevy, but we've been lucky enough to run the same car since 1973 without any major accidents or losses. We made some minor changes to the systems. For instance, we installed a reverser so we can back up like the Funnies do without needing a guy to push. That helps a lot when you have a small crew like we do. With the reverser, if we get on a track where the traction isn't as good as we want it, having a reverser lets us take longer for burnouts."

And another addition has been an aluminum engine Larry received for his 1977 campaign. It was Pat's contribution, a Christmas present to her husband. "He was really surprised and it was one of the most exciting gifts I made to my family. I felt we needed that kind of engine.

80

Just about everyone put aluminum engines in during the mid 1970s and ran better, so I felt we had to have one too."

From 1974 through 1976, the Dixons had a fair share of high spots. Larry made it into the fives in many runs and won some important second-level events, such as Fremont Raceway's East versus West Fuel Championships and the ninth annual Nitromethane Championships at Orange County Raceway. He also won a number of match races at United State tracks and, during 1976, at a number of Canadian strips during a very successful north-of-the-border tour.

But the race that still seemed most memorable to Larry in 1977 was his upset win at the 1970 Winternationals when young Larry, Jr., won such attention from TV viewers around the country.

"At the time, we were so happy just to qualify I don't think we thought much ahead to the eliminations until I was in the staging lane against Jim Paoli. He was a well-known driver, so it was a great feeling when I beat him in the first round. But then I was up against James Warren, whose name had been in the record book more than once over the years. Our luck held, though, because he broke his clutch and gave us a single.

"Then things got rough. I went all out to eliminate Ronnie Hampshire in the next round and we melted a piston on the run. We didn't have a spare of our own and we thought that was it. But drag-racing people are wonderful about helping each other. Jerry Johansen had an engine from an old Rattler along and he offered to let me use it. But it wasn't a bolt-in deal. When we started installing it, we found there were a lot of things that had to be done to make it work. So all of us began frantically running around to get spare parts from other drivers while the minutes kept ticking away. We were all sweaty and worried about whether we could complete everything before we had to be back on line for the next round. Everyone who could, pitched in to help us, but to this day, I don't know how we made it."

When the call came to enter the staging lane for round three, the

Dixon family was ready. Larry knew he faced another big challenge as he looked over to where TV Tommy Ivo's crew was getting their dragster prepared for burnout. Larry completed his own burnout and soon both drivers jockeyed to see who would stage first. Finally they both edged forward enough to light the amber on the Christmas Tree and both hit the gas pedal. But Ivo was a fraction of a second too soon. His car shot forward before the green came on. The red foul light came on in Ivo's lane, but all was green and happy on Dixon's side as he coasted down the strip to another win.

Now Larry found himself in the finals of a national championship event for the first time in his career. That alone was a major achievement, meaning good prize money and an increase in driving stature even if he lost the last race. But he and Pat daydreamed a little about what it might be like to reach the finish line ahead of Tony Nancy, their last competitor, while the TV cameras relayed the triumph to all corners of the nation. They hardly dared to believe it might come true, for Tony Nancy was another driver with a history of major accomplishments.

This was reflected in the relative attention paid the two teams by fans, reporters, and cameramen. "Tony Nancy had a good-sized crew. His cars always were immaculate and before the last run, everyone was interviewing him. Us little no names had a car that didn't have a fancy paint job, didn't have a lot of people helping us and nobody knew we were there. But even though the odds were against us, we meant to put up a fight and do the best we could."

Once again the two cars went through the ritual of burnout and the psyching attempts as the drivers inched toward the starting line. Then all at once the ambers were on and both cars blasted ahead down the track, the roar of the engines drowning the rising crescendo of yells from the crowd. It was not the time for babying the car, all the marbles hung on this single seven-second pass. Larry had the accelerator pedal down to the floorboard and could tell he had a slight lead over Nancy at the half-way mark.

"But it took its toll on the engine. I melted a piston at the three-quarter mark and globs of oil shot back over my helmet and goggles. I couldn't see where I was going, couldn't tell who was in front, but I drove the best I could and when I knew I'd passed the finish line I hit the chute button. When the car slowed down, I looked around to try to see where Tony was, but I couldn't make anything out. At first, I didn't see anyone rushing towards me and I didn't hear any noise, so I thought maybe I got beat.

"Then suddenly my wife came on in the push car with the horn blowing and I could see Keith Jackson coming my way and I figured we'd won. Then Larry, Jr., was in my arms looking at my face and asking whether I was hurt. While Keith tried to interview me, little Larry kept sobbing and saying, 'My daddy has oil all over his face.' "

At last, the happiness of his parents got through to Larry, Jr., and he relaxed and smiled a little. After Larry, Sr., answered Jackson's last queries, father and son nestled in the dragster cockpit, and little Larry raised his fingers in the victory sign as the car rolled slowly past shouting and applauding fans while the sun set in the west to end a demanding but perfect day.

5

Top Fuel Superstars

From the mid 1950s to the mid 1970s, the exploits of Don Garlits tended to overshadow all else in top-fuel racing. But there never has been a lack of great talent capable of challenging Big Daddy or anyone else for major honors. In fact, excellent as Garlits has been, he never could "win 'em all."

In the NHRA world champion point totals, for instance, other drivers, such as Don Prudhomme, Gary Beck, and Richard Tharp, consistently edged out Garlits for the crown in every year except 1975. A glance at the record book shows many other achievements by many colorful competitors, from TV Tommy Ivo to John Wiebe, Jim Nelson, Richard Tharp, and Shirley Muldowney. And there are names that do not show up very often on winning drivers lists who have had great impact on the sport—top-flight crew chiefs, engine designers, and car builders and innovators like Leonard Hughes, Ronnie Capps, and Mickey Thompson. The honor roll of top-fuel contributors is lengthy and interesting.

In the 1960s the name Don Prudhomme was one to be reckoned with in the field. Like many drag-racing stars, he grew up in Southern

California. He was born there in 1941 and attended local elementary and high schools. He was already interested in hot-cars in his teens and showed signs of coming greatness before he became twenty. As he told a reporter, "When I was 19 and just out of Van Nuys High, I belonged to a car club called the Road Kings of Burbank. Boy, I thought they were really a hot dog bunch then. Every Sunday we went out to San Fernando Drag Strip and raced whatever we could get our hands on."

Before long Don graduated to professional ranks. At the age of 21 he startled the drag world by traveling to Bakersfield, California, where he beat many of the best known drivers in the sport, taking first place in the Smokers meet for Top Fuelers. It was the beginning of a steady string of superlative top-fuel performances that made him one of the most feared drivers in the class, considered every bit as good as Big Daddy.

In short order Prudhomme won the nickname of "The Snake." He was driving the Black-Green-Prudhomme Special and sometimes went through months of competition without losing. A frustrated opponent quipped, "You're like a snake in the grass." Indeed, there is something of that feeling when one looks at the slender 6 foot 1 inch frame of the 165-pound Prudhomme. When he moves toward the cockpit of his present love, the Funny Car, he makes onlookers sense a coiled energy ready to be unleashed at unwary rivals.

Prudhomme once told Shav Glick of the Los Angeles *Times,* "I really hated that when it first started. I was ready to punch anybody in the nose who called me 'Snake.' But today I love it. I realize how much it's meant to me in publicity."

But it's a nickname well earned, because as the 1960s unfolded, Prudhomme struck again and again, always staying in contention in major meets and winning a good share of major titles. At the prestigious United States Nationals at Indianapolis, over a six-year span from 1965 through 1970, the Top Fuel class seemed to belong only to Garlits and the Snake. Garlits won twice in 1967 and 1968, but Prudhomme

**The Prudhomme Specials like this one struck fear into top fuel rivals in the
'60s.**

won three times, in 1965, 1969, and 1970. (Mike Snively was the other winner in 1966.)

The Snake won elsewhere too, taking first place at the Springnationals of NHRA in Bristol, Tennessee, in 1967; the 1965 NHRA Winternationals at Pomona, California; as well as dozens of other lesser ranked meets and championship events of other sanctioning bodies.

During the late 1960s it really was Prudhomme who had the best claim to being king of the Top Fuelers. He was top point driver for NHRA world champion several of those years, years in which Big Daddy had to settle for an also-ran position behind the redoubtable Snake.

Coming into the 1970s, though, the Snake decided to concentrate on Funny Cars. He pointed to his great success in Top Fuel in late 1970 and suggested he wanted new fields to conquer. "I won my share of nationals with dragsters, but I've never won a major title in a Funny Car. I want to win one and I think we have the car that can do it. I started driving Funny Cars as an exhibition-type thing, but now I'm serious about the challenge." Prudhomme, of course, was right. He soon became the winningest driver in Funnies, but that's another story—told in *Here Come the Funny Cars*.

The saga of Tommy Ivo isn't quite as spectacular as Prudhomme's, but it has some twists and turns quite different from the Snake's and some stellar achievements as well. If Ivo's story reads a bit like a movie script, that seems proper, since he has a legitimate claim to dramatic roots.

California also is the backdrop for Ivo's career. If the sun-drenched Los Angeles region is known as a hotbed of drag racing, it certainly is far better recognized as the movie/TV capital of the world. And show business first claimed the attention of Ivo (born in 1936) when he was still in elementary school. He demonstrated talent as an actor while a small boy and at the age of ten already was appearing with first-rank professionals. Thus an announcement released on April 10, 1946, read,

"Players' Productions will introduce a new 10-year-old child star, Tommy Ivo, when *On Borrowed Time,* starring Boris Karloff, opens at El Patio Theater tomorrow."

Tommy's acting career blossomed thereafter. He was given a number of parts in movies and then switched to TV where he was featured for some time in the "Margie" series. As is the case with many boys, he became interested in automobiles and racing at an early age and could hardly wait to get his driving license when he reached the legal age, 16 in California. A short time later he got his first dragster and the shape of his future was determined.

For some time drag racing was a hobby. He puttered around with his cars in between acting assignments and raced whenever he could. His driving skill improved steadily. Though he had the nickname of "TV Tommy" with the racing clan, they respected his ability. He was still making his living as an actor in 1960 when he made his first dent in the record books. He was running a twin Buick engine dragster at Pomona when he made everyone sit up and take notice with a dazzling run that clocked an e.t. of 8.95. That made him the first drag racer in history to break into the eights (that is, under nine seconds) on gas.

In 1962 TV Tommy added another notch in his belt at the San Gabriel strip. He roared down the track in 7.99 seconds, thus becoming the first driver from the West Coast to hit under eight seconds. It wasn't an official record, but it was below the recognized NHRA mark at the time, which was well up in the eights. The NHRA record didn't dip below eight until Bobby Vodnik clocked 7.96 in May, 1964.

Racing became more and more engrossing for Tommy until, in 1967, he had become a full-time driver who did some acting on occasion. He didn't win any national championship events, but he was always a threat and often got into the elimination rounds at major meets. He won his share of prize money in the other competitions, though, traveling from one end of the country to the other on the national tour.

Tommy enjoyed what he was doing and was popular with the fans.

89

But the years went by without anything happening to set him apart from many other top flight drivers. Then came a fall day in New Alexandria, Pennsylvania. The date was October 22, 1972, and things were going well for the Burbank ace. The engine in his dragster was revving smoothly and his times were about as close to the six-second level as any driver had achieved.

"It was one of those days you dream about," he recalls. "It started out warm in the morning and then the clouds rolled in, so the pavement was still hot, but the air was heavy. When the air is cool and heavy, the engine can produce more horsepower, but usually when that happens you can't get enough 'bite' out of the track. I had a run of 6.02 earlier in the day and went out to back it up. Everything went together perfect."

Indeed it did. TV Tommy left the starting line as if shot from a cannon and bought onlookers to their feet as he blazed down the quarter mile. There was a feeling in the air that something unusual was happening. The crowd roared approval when the announcer verified it. Tommy Ivo was the first driver to break the six-second barrier, achieving an e.t. of 5.97. It was the incentive for Cragar to start its Five-Second Club, with TV Tommy the first member.

When Tommy made that notable run, the only woman in the top ranks of professional drag racers, Shirley Muldowney, wasn't in position to become a Cragar charter member. Not that she wasn't racing well at the time; but she was driving Funny Cars. By the mid 1970s, though, she had swung back to Top Fuel, her first love in drag racing, and soon was the first of her sex to run in the fives.

Shirley, who grew up in Mt. Clemens, Michigan, got behind the wheel of a racing car almost as soon as she learned to drive. Her husband, who was in drag racing and was her mentor, started her off in stock classifications working up to a 1963 Super Stock Plymouth. But she wasn't very happy about driving a car with an automatic transmission. It just seemed too routine for racing. So she got him to build her a dragster which she drove for several years, often hitting speeds of 180

Looking more like a model than a drag racer, superstar Shirley Muldowney tests out the seat of her new dragster.

or 190 mph, before moving over to Funny Cars. She always liked dragsters better; they seemed to provide more excitement and challenge for her, but the growing popularity of Funny Cars indicated that class might be a good way for Shirley to build a reputation.

It wasn't an overnight thing, partly because she found a not un-expected opposition on the part of the sanctioning bodies to license a woman in one of the top three Pro classes. But the trim, 110-pound, pretty Mt. Clemens woman didn't get into drag racing by being a shrinking violet. She fought for her rights, insisting she should be judged solely on the merits of her driving ability. She gradually won over many male racers who helped convince NHRA, AHRA, and the other organizations that she deserved licensing.

Once able to compete on equal terms with other drivers, Shirley proved her case beyond a shadow of a doubt. From the start of the 1970s to mid-decade, she was a prime contender for Funny Car honors, a crowd pleaser and generally ranked among the top five drivers in that category. She took every danger the sport entailed in stride, calmly sitting out fires, spectacular crashes, and other hair-raising incidents, and coming back for more.

She always wanted to be judged on her merits, not her sex. It didn't seem to her to be praise when a driver who lost to her told an observer that "she drives like a man." Her acid response to that was, "Maybe one day, when he beats me, do you think they'll say, he drives like a woman?"

Shirley joined the top-fuel chase in 1974 in a Chrysler-powered rear-engine dragster. She didn't start winning championships right off, but with each meet her performances got a little better. Since she was the only licensed driver of her sex in Top Fuel, any time she set made her the fastest woman in Top Fuel. But she made run after run at speeds well over 200 mph and e.t.'s in the low sixes, which made her the fastest woman in all of drag racing.

During 1975, she became the first woman to join the sub–six-second

92

club with an elapsed time during one run of 5.91. Things were going well enough for her to plan to introduce a new car during the 1976 season, but delays in completing it forced her to use her old car for most of the major events. However, that didn't stop her. At the 1976 Springnationals in Columbus, Ohio, she qualified in a field that included almost every top driver in Top Fuel and then went on to send each one she raced "back to the trailer." On one run, she clocked 5.91 at 243 mph on the way to victory. When the smoke cleared, Shirley Muldowney had become the first woman to win a championship Top Fuel event of the NHRA.

In the fall, she had her new car and the racing fraternity awaited still more unusual achievements. Indications of what might be coming showed up soon. Shirley hit 6.02 twice at Seattle International Speedway and a little later turned in a 6.03 at Orange County Raceway. When she brought her "passionate pink" digger to the asphalt at Ontario that October, a sense of anticipation welled up in the crowd.

And she didn't disappoint them. She qualified with ease and then set a blazing pace through each elimination round. Every pass she made down the quarter mile brought cheers and "oohs" and "aahs" from the spectators as the public address system reported phenomenal times. On one run, she flashed through the time trap at a sensational 249.30, a speed that only Don Garlits had ever surpassed. As Shirley stormed to a first-place finish for her second major victory, she provided a series of four straight runs in the fives.

A few months later, the 37-year-old from Mt. Clemens demonstrated it was far from a fluke. At a track in New Mexico, she made a run in which she established herself as the fastest drag racer in the sport, a fantastic trip which recorded a top speed of over 252 mph.

It was a harbinger of things to come. The year 1977 was all Muldowney time. From the season-opening Winternationals at Pomona, where she set both low e.t. (5.85 sec) and top speed (248.61 mph) marks on, she set the world of drag racing on its ear by rapidly piling up

Two champions slug it out: hardly an eyelash separates the racers of Richard Tharp (near lane) and Shirley Muldowney at Englishtown, New Jersey, track. Tharp was NHRA world champ in 1976, but Shirley dethroned him in 1977.

enough points to turn the NHRA championship grouping into a shambles. She broke Don Garlits' Top Fuel world record, came out number one in the NHRA Summernationals at Columbus, Ohio, and the Summernationals at Englishtown, New Jersey, and finished the season the undisputed monarch of the top fuel arena. Once the fastest woman racer, now she had to be called the world's fastest drag racer.

Mt. Clemens, Michigan, isn't too far from the Canadian border and Shirley has plenty of fans in the country to the north. But Canadians have some heroes of their own to cheer about, not the least being Gary Beck.

Beck literally "came from nowhere" to become a major force in top-fuel racing in the mid 1970s. When he first showed up during qualifying for the 1972 United States Nationals at Indianapolis, people asked, "Gary who?" after he managed to turn in a good enough time to make the elimination rounds. No one expected him to do much because he had only driven a top-fuel dragster for three weeks before that prestigious tournament. To the amazement of audience and drivers alike, Gary blasted his way to the Nationals crown, along the way clocking a 6.11 e.t. at 230 mph in his Chrysler rear-engine car.

Some thought it a freak occurrence, but it was only the beginning. Beck kept making the "name" drivers sweat for any win over him in major championships the rest of 1972 and throughout the first part of 1973. Then, back at Indianapolis again in September, he really came into his own. During qualifying, he blasted down the track at 243 mph to post a 5.96 e.t. The latter mark made him the fifth driver to join the Five-Second Club and both clockings were national records briefly. In the very first round, he found himself matched with Big Daddy. Refusing to be awed, the Canadian sent the American superstar back to the trailer with a 6.01 versus Garlits' 6.13. Moving right along after that, Gary outmatched all his other adversaries to take the Nationals crown for the second year in a row.

Beck started off 1974 in style by defeating Garlits again in the final eliminator round of the Winternationals at Pomona, California. It was an omen. Throughout the year, Beck was almost always there in the final rounds of national events. He triumphed at the Springnationals in Columbus, Ohio. Later he had the pleasure of taking ovation after ovation from his countrymen in Montreal, Canada, as he won every round to clinch Top Fuel honors in the Molson Grandnationals. Though he didn't win every event, something few drivers in the hotly contested Top Fuel division ever came close to doing, he kept adding steadily to his point totals. When the season ended, he ranked as world champion, a pinnacle few drivers could claim after 5 or 10 years top-fuel racing, much less only a few years.

Gary didn't slack off during 1975 either, but he found himself facing stiffer competition from Don Garlits who avenged his 1974 Winternationals loss by coming in first in that leadoff meet. From then on, it was nip and tuck in the point totals. Garlits won the Montreal Grandnational and the United States Nationals at Indy while Beck took the first Fallnationals meet at Seattle International Raceway.

In addition, Beck won enough local or regional events to hold a lead over Big Daddy even though Garlits was victorious at more nationals. Garlits closed the gap in the early fall by coming in first at the Winston World Finals at Ontario Motor Speedway, California, but as the final NHRA competition approached in late fall, the Supernationals at Ontario, Gary held a slim edge in world championship points.

Feelings ran high in both camps. Garlits, who saw his chances for a first-ever NHRA crown growing dim, challenged some of the points awarded his rival. He went so far as threatening court action to invalidate what he felt were some unfair awards to Beck. But the final shoot-out occurred where it belonged—on the track—and this time Big Daddy could not be denied as he set a blistering pace that included new world's records in e.t. and in mph (the latter the first over 250 mph run) to capture the meet and the championship. The final Pro point totals were: Garlits, 9,693, to Beck's 8,990. Gary had nothing to be ashamed of. He had finished second to a legend and had shown his heels to everyone else, ending up more than 3,000 points ahead of third-place finisher Marvin Graham.

Going into the 1977 season, Beck seemed on the way to creating a legend of his own. He had a total of career runs in the fives only a little behind that of Garlits with the likelihood he'd pass Big Daddy by the time his career was over. During qualifying at the Winston World Finals of 1974, he had ripped down the asphalt at 5.69 e.t., the only man other than Garlits to have broken the 5.70 barrier. And he was ahead of Big Daddy in total fives run at NHRA national events.

Often making Big Daddy, Beck, and other superstars take notice over the years was the pride of the state of Washington, Jerry Ruth. No shrinking violet, he always called himself "King of the Northwest" almost from the moment he began to compete successfully in his home territory. He started building up a local following in the Washington area in the early 1960s and soon seemed almost unbeatable on his home tracks.

When NHRA instituted its divisional championship classifications in 1965, Ruth was the first winner and the record book shows he held almost a stranglehold on that division over the next decade. In the 10-year period from 1965 through 1974, Ruth was top point man in division six 8 out of 10 times, losing only to Larry Hendrickson in 1967 and Herm Petersen in 1974. In one year, 1972, he not only was division leader in Top Fuel, but in Funny Cars as well, taking 9 out of 10 possible meet victories.

For much of his career Ruth tended to stay close to home. Because he didn't travel a lot, he didn't have the odds in his favor to win the few major national events he attended. So for a long time he wasn't very well-known outside his own region, although he did bask in the national spotlight for a while in late 1966 when he held the national Top Fuel speed record with a 218.44 mph set at Arlington, Washington, during October.

Jerry Ruth in one of his '70s draggin' chariots. During one run at English-town in 1977, Ruth clocked an astounding 255.68 mph.

The old cliché about a driver not winning the big ones made the rounds in the late 1960s and early 1970s. But Ruth, who was expanding his touring efforts in the early 1970s, changed that tune in Amarillo, Texas in the fall of 1973. With his AA/FD rear-engine Chrysler digger turning over smoothly and powerfully, he outfought the cream of top-fuel racing to take the NHRA Winston World Finals. His winning marks were 6.11 e.t. and 232.55 mph. On January 27, 1974, Jerry became the eleventh driver to make the Cragar Five-Second Club with a mark of 5.95 seconds at Phoenix, Arizona.

As of the mid 1970s, few other racers had dominated their Top Fuel division the way Ruth had the Northwest, with one possible exception. Making a run for it was James Warren of Bakersfield, California. The veteran from the city known as "Nashville West" to country music fans took a little longer to establish his domination than his Washington rival. Warren was a popular figure at many meets in the 1960s, often doing very well, but not sweeping many events until the 1970s.

Though he didn't win his division in 1966, he held for a while the national record for quickest time, thanks to a 7.38 e.t. set at the Irwindale track that September. A year later, he took his hemi-head Chrysler dragster to a speed mark of 227.85 at Irwindale, enough to earn him a tie for the national record with Mel Van Niewenhuise. In January, 1968, Warren won his first NHRA national event when he finished first in the Winternationals at Pomona, California. But he still didn't have enough regional accomplishments in any of those years to take the division.

Once he got started, though, he was hard to stop. He won the NHRA Top Fuel championship in the Southwest Division in 1972 (the division includes California, Nevada, Arizona, Utah, and Hawaii). He then repeated in 1973, 1974, and 1975. In 1975, for instance, no one ever came close to his 3,133 point total. The nearest competitor, Frank Bradley, compiled a total of only 1,826.

Though Warren was the king of his region in the first half of the

99

1970s, he wasn't able to capture any national events. But he came close a number of times and he always was a threat to the best in the field. In 1974, for instance, he was the qualifying leader for the Winternationals with a 5.94. (The previous year, he became the sixth member of the Cragar Five-Second Club with a mark of 5.97 seconds achieved at Fremont, California, on October 13, 1973.)

Warren took part in the quickest side-by-side race in the history of the sport. It occurred in the second round of the 1975 Winston World Finals when he took on the driver then leading in championship points for the year, Gary Beck. In a race that left the fans limp, Warren roared down the strip in 5.80 seconds. But Beck went a hair faster, covering the distance in 5.74 seconds and nosing out the Bakersfield act at the wire. Thus Warren had the dubious honor of being the quickest loser in drag racing.

While this book is primarily concerned with championship elimination, there's another aspect of the sport that goes back to its early roots: match racing. In effect, match racing means that one driver challenges another to one race or a series of races. Most drivers enjoy that kind of racing. For one thing, you can choose the driver to compete against rather than depending on the luck of the draw. For another, it can be more relaxing to know you'll be in the race rather than having to work your way through the qualifying grind.

Just about every driver tries some match racing, but some do more than others. A good example is John Wiebe of Kansas who has often piled up 100,000 miles a year just driving to raceways across the nation for one-on-one competition. Of course, the money for match racing doesn't compare to the purses drivers receive for finishing on top or in the final 5 or 10 drivers in a popular drag meet, but money isn't the prime motivation of a driver who runs "strictly for the fun of it." (Besides, a series of matchrace fees can prove more rewarding than a steady diet of finishing in lower eliminator brackets.)

Wiebe also competes at all levels of Top Fuel. In 1968, for instance,

Here, Bakersfield's pride and joy, Jim Warren, gets set for another 200-mph-plus run.

he was the West Central Division Champion in NHRA Top Fuel, doing well in local events though he won no major crowns. Throughout the 1970s Wiebe was a familiar figure at most national events, his relaxed demeanor and obvious driving ability making him one of the most popular racers on the tour both with fans and fellow drivers. Like many first-rank drivers in the extremely competitive Top Fuel field, he often made his way into the last round or two of major events only to be turned back either by a malfunction in his dragster or a superrace by the man in the other lane. But he finally had his day in the Spring-nationals in Columbus, Ohio, in 1973. While the crowd roared its approval, he streaked to victory in his Donovan-powered rear-engine dragster.

It looked like a possible superyear for the Kansas favorite. But misfortune struck when his car went out of control during a summer meet and smashed into another dragster. Wiebe survived the mishap in reasonably good shape, but suffered a broken leg that put him out of competition the rest of the year.

Injuries are a part of the sport and usually are taken in stride. In 1974 Wiebe was behind the wheel again, and the following year he captured his division championship for a second time, compiling a total of 2,017 points against second-place finisher Gary Beck's 1,690.

The driver gets most of the credit for drag-racing exploits—and rightly so. But often the names of the team sponsors are almost as famous. At many a race from the early 1960s on the attention of knowledgeable fans centered on the dragster that bore the logo Candies & Hughes on its elongated body. In this case, the names are of people who remain behind the scenes of this Houma, Louisiana, entry. Paul Candies is an ardent drag-racing fan who was sponsoring his own dragster in top-fuel competition from the early 1960s on. In the mid 1960s he was joined by Leonard Hughes, recognized as one of the best mechanics in the drag-racing business. As crew chief, he has played a major role in the emergence of Candies and Hughes as one of the highest regarded teams in the field.

There were, of course, lean years when cars broke down or didn't meet performance expectations, or serious accidents to drivers cast a pall of gloom over the operation. But both Candies and Hughes remained confident they had the know-how to make up for any problems. By the early 1970s the good times far outweighed the bad and, in 1974, the team could point to the NHRA South Central Division Championship with Dave Settles handling driving chores. (The previous year, Settles had been Division leader as driver for Candies and Hughes' prime competitor in the Division—the Dallas, Texas, based Carroll Brothers).

Things weren't as bright in 1975 when the Candies and Hughes entry didn't make it for Division honors. But the tide really turned in 1976 when Richard Tharp of Dallas took over as head driver. Tharp, who had been Division champ in 1969 for the Carroll Brothers, reclaimed the post in 1976 with the Candies and Hughes car. But he did far more than that. He made his team a prime competitor in events throughout the United States and Canada; when the final tallies were in, he ruled as NHRA World Champion for the year.

It should be emphasized again that there are major contributors to the sport whose names may not show up in the record books or in entry lists for major Top Fuel events. These are the innovators, people like Mickey Thompson, who think up new ways of assembling and building dragsters to reach new heights of thrills and performance. Thompson, as noted previously, is considered the pioneer of the slingshot-type vehicle that became the basis for the superfast Top Fuelers of the 1950s and 1960s. Though he concentrated his driving efforts after the early 1950s in such pursuits as an assault on the world land speed record, in motorcycle exploits or in long distance desert racing like the Baja 500, he continued to think of improvements in drag vehicles. He worked at devising better control systems, changing the chassis design for improved weight distribution, and the like. For a number of years he sponsored his own racing team with Southern California driving ace Danny Ongais as his man behind the wheel.

Richard Tharp sends smoke clouds swirling during one of his patented burn-outs that helped pave the way for winning the 1976 TFE championship.

Thompson continued to set an example of courage and willpower in his many high-speed driving attempts outside drag racing. Over the years his infatuation with speed resulted in hair-raising successes and equally devastating failures—mishaps that often sent him to the hospital with broken bones or painful burns. But though he had broken almost every bone in his body by the mid 1970s and was in his fifties, he still kept coming back for more and setting new marks, if not in drag racing, in other automotive areas. To date he has collected close to 500 world and national speed records.

Bouncing back from adversity was part of his philosophy of life. As he told a reporter, "I love being alive. That's why I have to be doing things all the time." He made that statement only a short time after he'd fractured several vertebrae in a desert motorcycle spill. Despite that, he said, "Yesterday I got on the bike that threw me out there. My wife was really cursing, but I'll be damned if that bike is going to beat me."

His name has mainly been known to professional drivers in the drag-racing field as well as local fans in his home region of Southern California. But it does show up in the list of winners of the very first Winternationals in Pomona in early 1961 and thereby hangs a tale.

At the time Thompson was sponsoring his own dragster team which had two superfast entries in the middle-size class. The lead driver was Danny Ongais, and as it turned out, both Ongais' car and the other Thompson vehicle qualified and made it to the finals. When it came to the finals, both Thompson cars were still in it, but there was no one to drive the second car. Thompson decided to drive it himself, and to everyone's amazement he zipped past Ongais in the X/Dragster-Pontiac to win the class.

Like many racing experts, Thompson has taken an active part in community activities and in helping youth for years. Besides working on developing a home to help boys in trouble, he has set up scholarships for boys interested in auto engineering. As he stresses, "Racing has been good to me. Kids don't realize the opportunities that exist in this country and I hope I can help some of them take advantage of them."

6

Behind the Wheel

Knowing about some of the great moments in an exciting sport like Top Fuel drag racing and the careers of a few of the drivers who've made the field what it is today makes a day at the drags more interesting. It would be even better, of course, if you got the chance to sit behind the wheel of one of these vehicles and send it roaring down the asphalt. Perhaps some day you may actually do that, but for the time being we can get a little of the feeling by making believe we're taking part in a championship race.

You've trucked your low-slung digger out to the track in the trailer and have done well enough in qualifying to make the elimination rounds. It's early morning and you and your crew members are out in the pits carefully checking out every part of the car, from fat, slick, black rear tires to the hulking engine that sits between the huge rear wheels.

In the pits is where you and the skilled mechanics that make up the vital elements of your team spend almost 99 percent of your time. Each time you go down the strip, it takes only 5, 6 or 7 seconds. Even adding in the time spent in getting ready to move into staging position, we're

The final burnout—next comes the flashing ride down the asphalt.

only talking about a few minutes, maybe only 10 or 20. But that's the tip of the iceberg. The time in the pits takes hours and hours; and before you even get to the pits, you've spent countless other hours back at home base constantly working and reworking the hundreds of parts which must mesh perfectly together to make a really competitive car.

So the morning hours go by on race day and the sweat pours down the shoulders and from the backs of everyone as the work continues. Precision instruments—micrometers, voltmeters, adjusting wrenches—all come into play to make sure everything checks out. The spark plugs must have the right gap, accurate to fractions of an inch. The pistons must fit properly in the housing as must the piston rings which make sure the fuel and lubricants don't mix as the engine generates the 1,500 horsepower needed to whip the car forward to a blinding speed in only a few hundred feet. The brakes must sit exactly right to generate maximum stopping force when the brake lever is pulled. Perfectionism never ends.

Though you've started early and worked long, you don't know where the time has gone. The hours just don't seem long enough to accomplish all the adjusting and checking you want to do. Feverishly you and your associates finish up the last items as the call comes through to get ready for your event. The dragster, which won't spring to life now until it's in the staging lane, is pushed into position at the end of a long line of cars. Now the seconds seem to drag as the cars ahead of yours slowly move up toward the final jumping-off point for the race strip. There are many kinds of cars in the parade: other Top Fuel rails; plastic-body Funny Cars with their make-believe shells propped up in the air to reveal the cut-down dragster body beneath; Pro stock cars for the third professional category; and all kinds of vehicles for the Sportsman classes from beetlelike VWs to gas-fueled AA dragsters.

There's time now to talk some last-minute strategy with the crew members, to make sure everything's in readiness for the all-important last minutes in the prestage and stage lanes. You want to know if the burnout compounds are ready, if there are any special considerations in driving the lane you've ended up with, if the hand-held radios of the crew are in good working order and tuned to the car communications set.

At last you're up front. The two competitors ahead of you are in their final staging process; suddenly a thunder of sound, fire and smoke erupt as the cars take the green and swiftly become rapidly dwindling dots in the distance. The tower announcer completes his call of that race and turns his attention to you and your opponent as your cars are moved over the last white line of the waiting lanes and turned 90 degrees to the left into the staging areas.

Now you can feel the butterflies rising in your stomach as you exchange last details, then move carefully into the narrow cockpit, your body encased in the dully shining protective aluminized fire suit. Your feet are shod in special multilayer boots, which like the suit, can take temperatures well over a thousand degrees without transmitting the searing heat to your skin in case of a fire. You pull on your special gloves and finally, when you've made a last-second inspection of the controls and the gages, you signal the others to put on your helmet and the face mask with the special breathing apparatus. Now nothing of your face can be seen from the outside except, if someone gets close, your eyes behind the fireproof goggles.

You shift around to make sure you're as comfortable as possible in your snug enclosure and make certain your hand can reach the shift level without problem. You fasten your lap belt, making sure the quick-release buckle is off to one side so you can't hit it accidentally when you're moving the controls. You glance down at the tachometer needle, positioned in the middle of the dash so that you can catch a glimpse of the revolutions per minute the engine is pulling, while concentrating on the starting light on the Christmas Tree and the black surface of the strip stretching ahead of you.

You've flipped the magneto switch and the engine has come to life,

Throbbing power, blinding motion, are the inherent sensations of drag racing.

the souped-up nitro mixture exploding in regular series in the cylinders to keep the eight pistons moving up and down to turn the crankshaft. The crackle and pop as the burned gases spew out the curved exhaust stacks behind you sound only dully through your protective clothing, though you know their reverberations are strong and loud from the way the spectators along the rail sometimes put their hands to their ears.

When the engine is running smoothly and the crew has made any needed last-minute fine-tune adjustments, it's burnout time. Before this point your crew and the other team have agreed on just how many burnouts each driver will make and the procedure involved. You've decided to make two while your adversary in the other lane only wants one. So you'll go first to make one burnout, then both will burnout about the same time and move right into the starting phase when those are over.

You know the burnout is a very important step. It's meant to clean all the dirt and grime from the tires to insure that nothing will get between the synthetic rubber and the asphalt. The burnout also acts to heat the rubber. Both of these actions insure much better traction, that is, good contact between tire and road, so the car will have the maximum amount of energy applied to shoving it forward.

There are various kinds of liquids used for this operation. Plain water can be used or special traction compounds made of combinations of chemicals. You and your team have selected a compound and the team members jockey you into position so the rear wheels are just behind a compound bed called a bleach box. The crew now takes bottles of the compound and spreads the liquid evenly over the bleach box. The car is pulled into the puddle and allowed to sit there for a moment. You get the go signal and rev up the engine, closely watching the tach needle until it's indicating just the right output. The thin pointer slowly rotates around the dial to 1,000 rpm, 2,000, 3,000, 4,000. You have the shift lever in high because you want a lower rpm when the tires spin.

At one time, Pro Top Fuel dragsters had only one shift position. But Don Garlits helped develop a good two-shift system, and since then, just about every digger uses that approach. You have one too, a high and a low position. The low position rotates the tires faster, upwards of 8,000 rpm and more, to get more of a push. You want that when you're starting a race, because it takes a lot of energy to get a car moving fast from a standing position. But you don't need that kind of a shove when you're taking the first short move to prepare the tires.

When the rpms hit the level you want, you hit the throttle and let your clutch pedal out. The job of the clutch, of course, is to link up the rotating output shaft of the engine with the system that makes the wheels turn. In a split second, the linkup is completed and with a shattering blast, you and your car shoot forward. You only run out a few hundred feet before hitting the brakes. Behind you, two long black tracks glisten on the asphalt. The crowd near the starting area shouts its appreciation as the gray-white clouds of smoke float up from the ground, encasing the back of the racer in a sheath of pulsating vapor. It's a spectacular sight that somehow conveys a sense of power and danger to the eager on-lookers.

In your runout you've used your many hours of experience to keep the car moving forward straight and true. The lines behind your tires look as if someone laid them out with a ruler. Now it's equally important to retrace your movement so that the car doesn't waver from the tracks. You don't want to move out of those all important lanes because otherwise you might pick up unwanted dirt and grime from the untreated part of the roadway.

To make sure you move back properly, two of your crew help out. One stands in front of your dragster and one behind. Their job is to exchange signals between them as you slowly back up telling each other how the car is moving. (A few years ago, most Top Fuel vehicles didn't have a reverse gear. Almost all professional drivers have this now, as does your well-cared-for digger). The person in front combines all the information and passes it along to you so you can turn the wheel a little bit this way or that way to keep the tires right on the burnout trail.

Now you're back behind the bleach box for the second burnout. With the tires good and clean, your main goal now is to heat them up a little more, so you use a low gear which will give higher rpm. Once again the crew pours the traction compound into the bleach box. This time, the crew in the other lane is in action as well, as both you and your opponent get ready for the last full burnout before staging. With a higher rpm, you know the tires will be turning at speeds well over 100 mph equivalent, so you have to be particularly careful about your clutch action.

For this "hard" burnout it's vital that you get the clutch pedal in just before the tires hook up. It takes a short burst of power to get the tires spinning, then you have to quickly disengage the clutch. You know that if the clutch is in when the tires hit high speed, there's a great danger of losing control. Should that happen, the car might veer to one side or the other or even go into a roll that would send you spinning crazily end-over-end across the roadway. Even with a fire suit on and that heavy steel roll cage around you, it's not something you'd care to experience.

But after doing hundreds or thousands of burnouts, starting with less powerful cars and working up to the superpowered Top Fuelers, a driver develops the reflexes that automatically take care of the steps involved. So the clutch goes in smoothly as the tires grab the roadway and you monitor your gages and adjust things during the operation so the engine doesn't go past the danger mark. If you get too many rpms on the powerplant, the result can be a quick move back "on the trailer" and a costly repair bill.

Once again the staccato bursts of exhaust and the swirling clouds rise around the strip, this time from both lanes. As the crew members take up positions for another backup motion, you know the moment of truth is almost at hand. You know there's a suited-helmeted figure doing the same thing you're doing right next to you, but you don't look to see how he's doing. Concentration is the name of the game in almost every step of this high-voltage sport. You keep your eyes riveted to your crew, because missing the slightest signal might mean wavering from the lane. That extra dirt on your tires might cost only a tenth of a second, but that could be enough to make you an also-ran.

Both burnouts have taken only a short span of minutes, but it seems longer than that. As you follow directions back to the prestage area your mind sometimes may have random thoughts of doubt or even fear. But when the car is poised for the big one, when you've got your controls back in forward gear and you're getting set to stage, worries disappear and the thrill and desire of competing take over. If you concentrated before, now is the time for superconcentration. You have to make sure that every move counts as you and your opponent take the last steps in the process of racing: staging and hitting the gas pedal when the Christmas Tree flashes the final starting signal.

The Tree before you has a series of lights, but you know only the last couple will be working for Top Fuel racing. There are four lights that will go on as you finish your count-down. One is the prestage, the next the stage light, and the last two the yellow-green. As you move your throbbing car forward by inches, the prestage tells you you're close to the electronic beam that turns on the stage light. You have some decisions to make now. For one thing, are you going to try to psych your opponent by delaying staging and trying to make him go first? Or is it better to move boldly into position and be ready to go the moment he stages?

There are several possible advantages to making the other driver stage first. A main goal, of course, is to make the opponent nervous. Or it might let you do some last second maneuvering so you keep your engine and tires hotter than the other car. On the other hand, all that strategy might backfire by your own last-second loss of concentration or by a loss of performance in your own car during the extra waiting period. And you also have to decide whether to stage "shallow"—that is, whether to control the car by a technique like bouncing the front

115

tires so the front end is just far enough into the stage zone to turn on the yellow light.

The point in staging shallow is that it keeps an extra 12 to 14 inches between the front of your car and the electric eye that turns on the red light for a foul start. And when that bright red light winks at you, you're through for the day. (Even if both cars redlight, you are well aware that if you redlight first, the other car is the winner).

Obviously trying to do a move like that just right can be tricky, even if you've done it countless times. Which is why special devices have been developed to aid you, like the Hurst Line/Loc system. This is a combination of electronics and mechanical controls that will automatically insure the staging position you want when you turn it on. The button which actuates the Line/Loc is located on the side of the shift stick where you can depress it with your thumb. In that position, once you've pushed the button down, it's a cinch for you to swiftly move the thumb away and have your hand free to operate the shift.

At the moment, your thumb hovers just above the button as you hold off to try to make the driver next to you make the first move. The two cars sit there, side by side, separated by only about 10 feet, with smoke and fumes eddying back from the idling engines. It takes an effort of will to keep from hitting the button to get things going. Every muscle in your body is tensed, waiting for the moment when the minutes and seconds of waiting turn into sudden action. You can almost feel the blood pounding through your veins as you sit in that strange enclosure in a world of your own. It's just you and your machines against all comers. The thousands of fans out there yelling themselves hoarse are as remote as if they were on Mars.

You feel the strain of waiting. The thought comes that perhaps it's your car that's losing its punch, your tires that are cooling, cooling, cooling until they won't grab the asphalt as you want them to. Finally, you decide you'll go first after all, when suddenly, from the corner of your eye you get a sense of movement. A light flashes on the Christmas Tree.

Your adversary has staged and now it's your turn.

You push the Line/Loc button and move your car just enough to light the stage bulb. As soon as you start this step, you crowd everything else from your mind. The next few seconds are the most crucial of the whole series of steps that lead you from the pits to that finish line a quarter mile away. The only thing that counts is seeing that single yellow go up on the Tree and reacting to it swiftly, instinctively, without a bit of waste motion. Just a lapse equal to the wink of an eye is enough to give your opponent the tiny edge he needs. For, as the saying goes in drag racing, "snoozers lose!"

If you've raced before, you've heard it before. As one of the best drivers, Tom McEwen puts it, "You have to leave on the yellow. The lights are so fast, and there's a gap of from four-hundredths to twenty-five–hundredths of a second between human reaction time and how long it takes the car to start moving forward. With that kind of time difference, if you waited for the green and the guy next to you went on the yellow, you'd get beat. If I've made a good burnout and everything's OK, the car will leave without spinning its wheels."

As you focus on the Tree, you have the confidence that shallow staging has given you an extra margin for error. Of course, the same might be true for the fellow in the other lane, but you can't worry about him. The vital thing is to get those engine rpms as high as it's safe to do, ready to give 'er the gun and go full speed ahead as soon as a glint of yellow shows up. For you know that it isn't who covers the quarter mile in the shortest time or who makes the highest speed that counts, it's which car pierces the electronic eye that is the invisible guardian of the finish line first. There have been countless cases where a driver leaves a tenth or two-tenths of a second late and is just nicked at the other end by a driver who alertly "stood on it" at the first glimmer of yellow. "Snoozers lose."

Suddenly, there it is! The yellow light blinks on and you hit it. There's a jolt as you take your foot off the clutch and hit the accelerator to make the tires squeeze the surface to propel you into the straightaway. You hold the wheel steady, though you know for the first few hundred feet there's not much that steering can accomplish. With almost all the weight of you and your car pumped into the rear wheel, the front end has so little force that it's almost floating. The key to a good straight start lies in past work, in careful honing of all parts of the car to insure stability and good weight distribution so the rail won't swerve to one side or the other and lose precious seconds.

And you also don't want to see that front end fly up in the air in a wheelie. That's a maneuver that looks spectacular, particularly with the long drawn-out shape of the Top Fuel dragster. It's fine for stunt drivers who give the crowd a thrill between races, but it slows the car down and eats up time. Like all good racers, you've done everything possible in the design of the vehicle and with your driving skills to keep those front wheels on the ground. If you leave the asphalt for a second or two during the first push forward into the strip, that's all right, but no more than that.

Now you're really barreling along, the speed rising rapidly toward the 200 mph mark. You keep your gaze fixed on the track and the finish line, ignoring what's going on in the next lane, at least until you shift gears. You know you're doing pretty well because there's no one way ahead of you, but you don't know if your adversary is behind you or sizzling along side by side. You only can be concerned with controlling your own rocket on wheels, making sure you keep your composure and listen to the changing tone of the engine. About half-way down the track, you hit the shift lever to high gear. At the "mid," the dragster has accelerated to a high enough speed so you don't need all the extra engine rpms to get the initial slingshot effect, so the shift brings the rpms down and helps protect the engine from burning out.

It's only been a few seconds since you shot forward from the starting line and already the race is half over. The sea of faces in the stands are a blur, the guard rail a vague outline to one side as you shoot ahead

118

toward the strip of slanting white lines that marks the finish area. Now you can take a fast glance to see where the other driver is. You feel a glow of satisfaction to find you have a few car lengths margin. You wait a second or two more to make sure, then start turning down the engine. As any good driver knows, if it looks like the race is won, the prime goal is to prevent damage to your equipment. If you keep the engine going at top performance right through the finish lights, you're gambling with a possible burned piston or a blown engine. And with more rounds to go in a meet, you don't want to have to change engines back at the pits.

Long before you've reached the finish line, you've taken one hand off the wheel and grasped the parachute release. As soon as you pass the front light of the speed trap, you hit the release. You can't see it, but the officials and crowd observe the pilot chute come free, followed a split second later by the main chute, which floats airily behind as you roar past the end light of the trap. Sensing the chute is out, you shift into low gear and actuate the engine shutoff. You apply your hand brake at the right time to bring the car to a final stop several hundred feet past the trap.

The last step in the shutdown process is switching the magneto off. You've waited a bit longer to do that to let the engine cylinders run dry of nitro so there will be no danger of fire now that the race is over.

You take off your helmet and hardly have you done that than the crew rushes up in the truck, holding their hands up in victory signs and shouting with glee. Swiftly they pitch in to fold the chutes and stow them, drain water from the engine and do the other last details to insure everything is shipshape. The tow bar is attached and you sit back to take the plaudits of the crowd as the car moves slowly down the return lane toward the pits . . . where work will start all over again for the next run.

Index

124

The Author

Irwin Stambler is a prolific author in the automotive and sports fields who has published many popular books with Putnam's. His most recent well-received book on drag racing was *Here Come the Funny Cars.* Others of his popular automotive books published by Putnam's include *Minibikes and Small Cycles, Great Moments in Stock Car Racing, The Supercars and the Men Who Race Them,* and *Automobiles of the Future.* Mr. Stambler lives with his wife and children in Beverly Hills, California.